Oxford Poets 20.

The editors of this anthology are members of the OxfordPoets Board.

IAIN GALBRAITH is a poet and translator and the editor of four previous anthologies of poetry. His recent books include a translated and annotated selection of poetry by W.G. Sebald, *Across the Land and the Water* (Hamish Hamilton, 2011). He lives in Wiesbaden, Germany.

ROBYN MARSACK is Director of the Scottish Poetry Library in Edinburgh. With Ken Cockburn, she co-edited the anthology *Intimate Expanses: XXV Scottish Poems 1978–2002* (SPL/Carcanet, 2004), and with Andrew Johnston, *Twenty Contemporary New Zealand Poets* (Carcanet, 2009). She lives in Glasgow.

Also available from Carcanet/OxfordPoets

Oxford Poets 2000
Oxford Poets 2001
Oxford Poets 2002
Oxford Poets 2004
Oxford Poets 2007
Oxford Poets 2010

Oxford Poets 2013

an anthology edited by
Iain Galbraith
Robyn Marsack

Oxford*Poets*

CARCANET

First published in Great Britain in 2013 by
Carcanet Press Limited
Alliance House
Cross Street
Manchester M2 7AQ

www.carcanet.co.uk

A CIP catalogue record for this book is available from the British Library

ISBN 978 1 90618 810 8

The publisher acknowledges financial assistance from
Arts Council England

Typeset by XL Publishing Services, Exmouth
Printed and bound in England by SRP Ltd, Exeter

Contents

Introduction   xi

Gregor Addison
Denny's Shipyard, Dumbarton, 1959   3
United Turkey Red   3
Bespoke (Loch Sloy Hydro Dam, 1948)   4
Slant   4
Stamford Hill   5
Pte 1091 Allison, aged 19   5
Past tense   6
Clydeside, March 2011   6
Till   7

David Attwooll
March for the Alternative   11
'SPEEDER CLAIMED CAR WAS DRIVEN BY HER DEAD MOTHER'   12
Message from an agnostic angel   12
Wiggy in Cornwall   13
Banner for Bid   14
Hyperlinks in Mesopotamia, Oxford   15
Morning in Chapultepec   16
The sound ladder   17
Flags in East Dulwich   18
Resurrection   18
Milvus Milvus   19

Emily Ballou
The Importance of Tea   23
Twenty-three pictures of the desert   24
I, Lizard, performance artist   31

Paul Batchelor
Brother Coal   35
Pit Ponies   37
from The Orchards (after Rilke)   38

Christy Ducker
from Grace Darling's ABC   45
from Grace Darling's Journal   48

Lynn Jenner

The Russian Point of View	53
I have a feeling with no name	57
For Maisie Brown	58
The hot early universe	59
Ten rules to guide me in my research	61
Six New Zealand Jews Share Their Impressions of Oświęcim	62
I'm not sure what to call what I have done	63
'In the voice of Paul Celan'	64

Riina Katajavuori

Elin	67
'I eat a pepper that's not'	67
Superimpositions	68
Fathers and sons	69
Ninety-One	70
'morning tree'	71
Beslan	71
Crow Grabs Poet's Scalp	73
In the forest, Hansel tells Gretel about owls	74
Self-portrait 18.3.2009, 1.20 p.m.	75
'From the windowed veranda'	75
'A boy reaches the monster island'	75
'I listened to the soundscape'	76
'The bewilderment that to other people'	76

David Krump

Notes from a Journey	81
An Ample Tree	81
Failed Sidekick's Dilemma	82
Prometheus at the Checkpoint	83
Love Song for Rural Idiots	83
Ophelia Soft	84
Poem Written in Realtime	85
One Crow	85
A Stream	86
Old Geometry	86

Frances Leviston

GPS	89
IUD	89
Kassandra	90
Bishop in Louisiana	92
Sulis	93
Woodland Burial	96

Peter Mackay
The Log Roller   99
Logorrhoea (Logorrhoea)   100 (101)
Na Dorsan (The Doors)   102 (103)
Bàta Taigh Bàta (Boat House Boat)   104 (105)
Ball-sampaill (Specimen)   106 (107)
An Tobar (The Well)   108 (109)

Ádám Nádasdy
Creation   113
Family Photo Album   113
Angel in the Next Underground Coach   114
On the Big Dipper   114
Take Down his Particulars   115
Better Staying Put   115
Silent Interval   116
Swaying Chandelier   117
One of My Paintings   117
Some Sort of Mirror at the End of the Room 118
Adam and Eve   118
Just Go!   119
Self-Portrait   120

André Naffis-Sahely
Blood and Proverbs   123
Augury   123
N16 8EA   124
Family Business   124
Auroville   125
Professional Vagabonds   126
An Island of Strangers   127
The Journalist Speaks of the Dictator   128
The Return   129
Forward March   129
Exile, Italian Style   130

Vivek Narayanan
Rama   133
Tataka   134
Rama's Servants   135
What the People Said   136
Chitrakuta   138
The Jewelled Deer   139

Leonie Rushforth
How to Get There 145
On the Ource 146
Janus Fleuri at the Freud Museum 146
Kairos 147
Fontenay 148
Mist Lifting on Mount Caburn 150
Gorky Park 151
Song for Carmen 152
You With Work To Do (*after Pushkin*) 153

Kerrin P. Sharpe
a possible journey 157
sewing the world 157
six lies for an orthopaedic surgeon 158
The Alchemy of Snow 160
three days in a wishing well 161
world without maps 162
because my father 163
In the cart 163
the rice planters 1953 164
the whistler 164
their faces turn pages 165
there are few sightings 166

Ian Stephen
In Breton 169
In Brest 169
Che Perig et Anna 169
Conversation on Ouessant 170
Blue Woman, Brittany 170
Crossing the Minch 171
A way of putting things aside 172
Sailmaker's whipping 173
Cape Farewell – Scottish islands voyage 174

Toh Hsien Min
At night's border with the next day 181
Quince 182
Airborne 184

Jan Wagner
anomalies 193
columbus 193

december 1914   194
tea bag   194
from 'eighteen pastries'   195
the west   196
the man from the sea   197
staniszów   197
blues in august   198
dobermann   198
chameleon   199
hops   199
meteorite   200

Karen McCarthy Woolf

Thirteen Names for the Moon   205

Introduction

This is the seventh Oxford Poets anthology since 2000, and our hope is that readers coming to an Oxford Poets anthology for the first time will feel inspired and heartened, as we have, by the passion and accomplishment of the work presented between its covers. Those who have enjoyed previous anthologies in the series will welcome the continued interrogation of the formal and thematic breadth in contemporary poetry, as well as the opportunity the present selection affords to discover new and compelling voices and explore some unfamiliar correspondences and perspectives. The format of the last anthology, in which the poet's biography and a short statement by each poet reflecting on his or her work preceded a sizeable selection of poems, has proved attractive to many of our readers: there cannot be a better argument for retaining it here.

Oxford Poets 2013 also follows previous anthologies in its openness to poetry's many localities and provenances. Poetry's diversity and exuberant vision resist containment by categories such as nation, gender or region. The present volume, open to poets from different continents and cultures, provides the appropriate environment for a kind of writing to which memory, breathing, space and silence have traditionally meant more than national or even linguistic affiliation. On receiving a copy of Rainer Maria Rilke's volume *Vergers*, collecting poems that he had written in French – some of which we present here in Paul Batchelor's graceful translations – Marina Tsvetayeva expressed to their author her surprise that anybody should wish to reduce poetry's dimension to a national province or the confines of a single language: 'Writing poetry is itself translating', she wrote, 'Orpheus bursts nationality, or he extends it to such breadth and width that everyone (bygone and being) is included'. While the work of a poet may bear the lifelong impress of a particular landscape, his or her *reading* is likely to see through borders. A poet living in Manchester, Mumbai, Basel or Adelaide probably will be as drawn to American, Spanish or Arabic poetry as to poetry written in his or her own region or dialect. Access to other poetries across economic, political or linguistic boundaries cannot be taken for granted, however, and this volume wishes to champion translation's service to the global republic of poetry. Moving beyond the paradigm of periphery and centre, *Oxford Poets 2013* focuses neither on English poetry nor poetry in English, but assembles the work of nineteen poets from a dozen different countries, with translations from several languages: Finnish, German, Sanskrit, Russian, French, Hungarian, and Scottish Gaelic.

The poems in this anthology associate by theme. A common thread links the many types and meanings of migration: sojourns in foreign places, new beginnings, journeys through real or imagined landscapes, translations between languages, cultures, codes, dimensions, and systems. Another strand foregrounds the beguilements and betrayals of memory: the siftings and shifting of its layers, excavation and archaeology, personal and public histories and archives, (mis-)information and myth. Many of our authors investigate a heritage of stories or records, others put language itself at the centre of their work: language heard from 'outside', language on reality's 'cutting-room floor', language 'in realtime'. Many find intricate forms for their poetry. More often than not, several such *topoi* are braided into one poet's work, in the rich mix of a single poem.

Gregor Addison's poems are like multi-dimensional maps 'where the local and the world meet'. Listening to family stories across the years is not only a way of 'locating' himself, but a pointer to other lives, tragedies, roads not taken. Listening plays a central role in David Attwooll's work, too. His celebrations of music have a unique brio; aware of a beat far below deck, his voyages are 'propelled by the sound of cellos'. His poems of family touch public history, and 'remembrance' is a word he is not afraid to use. Family stories can often be 'hidden histories', fragile in their battles with repression and invaded privacy, and Christy Ducker's abecedary sequence about the life of a reluctant celebrity finds a powerful and yet delicately respectful form to document her personal witness to the Grace Darling archive. Lyn Jenner confesses to being another storyteller, and her work – like that of Emily Ballou, Toh Hsien Min, Vivek Narayanan and other poets here – is untrammelled in its espousal of 'free' forms. She describes herself as 'a nerdy, archive-loving type in real life', but it is imagination rather than a library card that brings her to a remembering that will not be 'mere memory' (Jean Améry) and longs to 'make a new poem from the few words which, by chance, have survived the flames'.

Jan Wagner is one of German's most skilful contemporary poets; sonnets, sestinas, villanelles and Sapphic odes flow with ease from his hand. But his scintillating displays of classical form are balanced by 'surprise and transgression': poetry's 'bond with our steaming, glowing, odorous, noisy world'. Paul Batchelor's poems 'Brother Coal' and 'Pit Ponies' set out from a burning loyalty to class and family history, and yet writing them has brought him up against a productive paradox: poetry, he writes, 'wants all the loyalty for itself'. Rilke's French poems are less well known than his German ones, and we are glad to have Paul Batchelor's translations here. Translation, seeking its distance between the countenance of the source and the work-face of the new language, is always modernising, beginning, making it new, and Vivek Narayanan's research-driven renewal of the Sanskrit *Ramayana* shows the poetics of a translation masterpiece *in statu nascendi*.

'Who would be the archivist of last things', asks a poem by Emily Ballou; her generous, wide-ranging forms compose a 'score of human traffic', not forgetting the desert-inscribed glyphs and 'graffiti' of her invented character Lizard. Peter Mackay's work inhabits a 'trans-historical' landscape, criss-crossed by journeys between the modern metropolis of his working life and the Lewis of his younger years, recouped in poetic sorties in a language whose names and nouns contain the 'scorings of different cultures: Norse, Gaelic, Scottish, Anglo-Saxon'. The 'love of roaming' mentioned in André Naffis-Sahely's 'N16 8EA' has carried him to many distant places on the globe – distant from where? His 'life studies', a form some of these poems suggest, are as likely to invoke Persian Tus or the 'experimental' town of Auroville in Tamil Nadu as London's Stoke Newington, and yet each poem worries at a local catastrophe. Karen McCarthy Woolf's 'Thirteen Names for the Moon' sings the moon's moods, finding a haunting voice for a passage from bereavement to poetic resolution.

Journeys, especially sea voyages, as well as a seaman's tales of foreign places, appeal to Ian Stephen, whose poems are full of tacks and booms, crossings and compass points, lending an existential urgency to landmarks. 'Night crossings' and flight paths are central to the stepped forms of Toh Hsien Min, but the view from the port-hole does not always reveal reliable points of orientation: 'you can only see this / from a distance: / the fist of clouds, / those leakages of light, / twitching electricity'. Invention's negotiations with memory, as well as 'meetings and sightings', mark Kerrin P. Sharpe's lyrical paths through a 'world without maps', while Leonie Rushforth's tentative surveyings detail instructions for transit: 'writing a poem is usually a process of making my way somewhere I can't get to using normal navigational instruments like thought or conversation'. Frances Leviston's poetic dissection of disinformation would put the theodolite of the poem itself on trial – along with that *'jar in Tennessee'* ('IUD') that can render a wilderness 'no longer wild'.

Suspicions about the 'questionable truth' (Leviston) of poetry preoccupy David Krump, too, who, in an auto-da-fé of self-irony, puts the finger on the 'cartoonishly ... manageable' experience contained in 'margins, borders, beginning and ends'. His poems are tight, to be sure, but leave plenty of space for the pitfalls and swings they so deliciously invoke. Riina Katajavuori's work surprises us with 'strange encounters ... and all sorts of unrelated events and objects', not only in her native Finland, but in places as far apart as Fair Isle (Shetland) and Budapest. When Ádám Nádasdy, from Budapest, describes himself as 'no innovator' and his subject matter as 'unpoetic', it hardly sounds like a recipe for bliss. And yet all of his poems are just that: celebrations of the piercing longings and 'unexplained hopes' of the quotidian and commonplace, which may assume unexpected guises: 'doorknobs, tram drivers, or God serving me dinner'. Poetry! Can life do better?

We, at any rate, could not have done without the prescient advice and enthusiasm – while this volume was still on the drawing-board – of our Oxford Poets co-editor Jeremy Noel-Tod. We have had great pleasure in sifting these poems and corresponding with their authors, and hope that readers will find much to please, surprise and pique their interest in these pages.

Iain Galbraith
Robyn Marsack
February 2013

GREGOR ADDISON was born in Dalkeith in 1966 and raised in Alexandria and Clynder. He worked as a chainman/labourer until he was twenty-two, then went to Newbattle Abbey College where he studied Philosophy and English Literature; from there to Aberdeen University, studying English Literature and Gaelic; then to Jordanhill College. He teaches English at Clydebank College.

Harold Pinter once said that, at some point, the world and your world must meet. For a long time it seemed to me that life was lived elsewhere; why would I write about where I live? What is there to say? But I gradually saw that the push and pull of historic changes might be read in the working lives and movement of my own family members. Families tell stories – not all of them true, perhaps – and for some of the poems here I was torn about how much of the truth should be in them. Did I even have a right to tell the stories? I reminded myself that these stories have been passed down through many re-tellings and I suspect they have been shaped many times before they even got as far as my ears. The poems that appear here are not just a way of locating myself – though they are certainly that – but they point to other lives lived, to abandoned dreams and personal tragedies.

My immediate world is the west coast of Scotland, particularly the area around Loch Lomond, the Gareloch, and extending all the way to Glasgow. Balloch and Dumbarton are where my parents were born and I can't help but remember two stories told to me over the years. In the late 1940s, my mother was taken on a walk up a local coffin road known as the Staney Mullan, which offers views over Loch Lomond and the Vale of Leven. My mother's uncle had a small portable radio and this was playing Edith Piaf's 'La Vie en Rose'. Still a child, my mother looked down on Loch Lomond and its many islands and thought she was looking out upon Canada and Australia. The second story is one my father recently told me and involves another local place, the Dumbarton Crags – a volcanic ridge that runs along the hills above Dumbarton. As a boy, my father used to sit with his father listening to Conan Doyle's *The Lost World* on the radio. Later, up on the Crags, he'd imagine this was his lost world. At some point, the world and your world must meet; sometimes, it occurs through a child's imagination; sometimes, through the need for employment that forces us to travel. Many of these poems are about the points at which the local and the world meet through various individuals' experiences.

Denny's Shipyard, Dumbarton, 1959

Boiler-suited, cap and tools wheeling like crows,
a pillow burst like flak, or black feathers
falling, clawing the air like Icarus.
The rigging gave, cracked like a nut. One slow
agonising moment and another –
the hull wrong way up like a steel cathedral.
Still we like to think he did not suffer.
But he held on for days in that hospital.

In Curaçao or Port Sudan, father felt the cargo
shifting in the hold. Surely an omen?
The women brought the body home, and began
the mourning – cursing the man
who felled the one thing in life you could cling to.
Who orphaned the postcards you'd send back home.

United Turkey Red

So my forefathers and their offspring fled
the famine in Tandragee, the arse-end
of Ireland. The roughers slammed the docks, splashed
their cold thin faces (red as madder, fixed
in alum mordant). Paddy's Milestone had smalled
to one pale rock and the day ran like ink
on an envelope. In a carryall
they'd stowed their bric-à-brac, their shawls, strong drink
to lift their dampened spirits. For wasn't theirs
a one-way trip? Except, they'd never lose
their feel for home-spun histories, would weave
new fabric worked in blood into a shared
memory. New worlds loomed, new prints and hues
of India. Soaked calico stained their sleeves.

Bespoke (Loch Sloy Hydro Dam, 1948)

Crushed stone from Ben Vane vibrates the conveyor
as mother takes tiny, measured steps, making
small alterations to fall in behind
her father, the tailor, who worries the tape like a rosary.
In dirt and dungarees, the men look up and shake
their heads to loose the sweat. Half-blind
from concrete dust, cursing their luck, their history,
they dam all with a shrug of round, taut-muscled
shoulder. The tailor unpockets a notebook
making pencil sketches for an inventory,
as the Polish foreman (made-to-measure) is hustled
into thoughts of how he'll look
come pay day. Fingering samples, giving a brusque
but non-committal nod to the cloth-blue dusk.

Slant

A flat top trunk, a packer lugged Stateside
in the 20s, sits by the window,
bearing the scars from the gangplanks grandfather
                           dragged it down.
The stevedores rough-housing pitted its face
like an overripe avocado, spooned out
its secrets, until it finally passed to me to prove
some stories come at you pitched at a slant.
It weathered depressions,
languished in basements, a greenhouse, a shed.
Then glossed over, settled in an alcove for years
without incident. It is
in its solid, dogged way, a statement. A testament
to the everyday, stowed away with fragile dreams
in its papered womb, in its empty chest.

Stamford Hill

Then in the closing 50s, the rivers of blood were a spring
just gurgling. At the registry office, Stamford Hill,
my parents married, having shunned the ill-
will of religion.
Now, salt-beef bagels became my father's obsession.
He'd croon Sinatra. And in the Kosher baker's
on Dunsmure Road, they dubbed my mother Cleopatra.

Next door, the old executor (who'd escaped the Baedeker
Blitz on Exeter to his London bed-sit) played
Beiderbecke on an old Dansette – as if
those Afro-Caribbeans had not yet left the MV *Empire
Windrush* with their own swung-rhythm.
The Broadway drew Hasidic Jews in evening amber
and time was of no matter, the ebb and flow
of lepers, of pilgrims, little more than a side-show.

Pte 1091 Allison, aged 19

She cradled the tin box, worn and rusted
as an urn for ashes. Six decades dead,

her older brother decayed in her last days
until all that was left was this shared grief,

a soldier in a photograph, chest out, stood
to attention. Private 1091 Allison

stopped with one shot, a line of sight pointing
to the front room in a Dumbarton pre-fab,

a sofa thinned with sitting, stained red and soft
as a paper poppy. Some sniper that, to inflict

a wound that would weep a lifetime and more,
to encompass us in the scope of his lone rifle.

Past tense

Tungsten-warm, a lemon strip illuminating
the horizon, awaiting the patter
of morning rain on an old zinc roof. Later,

trying to fathom the depth of days, their drop –
stopping to gaze up at Beinn na Caillich,
a moment's longing sharp on the tongue.

Sat on the bench with a dry book, I parse
her words precisely, sensing
their bitter afterbite, the pith and rind.

Clydeside, March 2011

Slowly, like wet swarth, silvered and lathered,
the river wanders and a boat passes,
and a bow-wave bellies up, out, like blown glass.

Here, in '36, the Great Queen shipped
out into the world to whistles, cheers, drawn
by the tracer's celluloid hand, and slipped

her hatching ground. Spawned in the squat shadow
of the great crane. Titan, spurned, overthrown,
looks idly on at boats that pass below.

Where riggers fell, now daffodils push up, massed
at the water's edge where memory washes.
And turn their heads with the sun that passes.

Till

I've known exposed till, soft ground returning
footsteps with a sprung rhythm. I've scaled spoil
and scree, running upwards against churning,
slipping stone, defiant over the shale-oil
lacquered slopes. Round-calved, I've laboured sand dunes,
trod for miles over sinking bog, weary,
tired, but happy all the same. Whistled tunes
when the sun was full and rubbed at bleary,
sleep-filled eyes in long hours idled with friends.
The winter wash is clearing the moraine.
I've set up home, alone, almost content,
with walls for old memories; the telephone
asleep in its cradle. The sills have silted.
I'm living at an angle now, stilled, tilted.

DAVID ATTWOOLL lives in Oxford where he works in publishing, and plays drums in a street band. His poems have been published in various magazines; of those included here, 'March for the Alternative' first appeared in *Magma*, 'SPEEDER CLAIMED CAR…' in *Rialto*, 'Wiggy in Cornwall' in *Smiths Knoll*, and 'Banner for Bid' in *The Reader*. Grateful acknowledgements are due to the editors of those magazines.

I wrote poetry (and lyrics) as a student, as you do; then for forty years didn't. I'm a late starter: a resolution to do something new each month of the year I reached 60, four years ago, produced (along with a hilarious tango class, inept yoga, etc.) an attempt at a sonnet. Evening poetry classes followed, and I have been very lucky to have had a stellar roster of mentors who kindly guided and encouraged me – Giles Goodland, Gerard Woodward, Jane Draycott, George Szirtes, and Jenny Lewis.

My preoccupations are commonplace: time and memory; the sea; processes in low- and high-tech media; half-understood science and the mysteries of the brain; local histories; politics (with a small p); death (inevitably); light and sound. And especially music. I've been an amateur drummer since my teens and that must nudge both the way I write, pushing against form and syntax, and what I write about. I try to listen out for what the rhythm section is doing beneath the surface melody of places and events, the beat a few strata down.

Our street band played (a ragamuffin mix of jazz and 'world music') on the anti-cuts 'March for the Alternative' in March 2011, and as well as the politics there was something ancient and ritualistic going on there. 'Flags in East Dulwich' is based on true family stories; 'The sound ladder' was sparked by the mongrel cross of a South American anthropological exhibition in Paris and Nordic musicians playing ice instruments in Oxford. I have a weakness, I realise, for secular resurrections. Generally, I hope I've been courteous enough to leave doorways open in the poems (as Paul Farley put it), so they don't need any gloss here.

Of course all they are really 'about' is the process of grappling with language. I love the fact that in Greek airports a *metaphor* is the conveyor belt carrying our overstuffed suitcases around: there's the odd business of making things less familiar to try to perceive them afresh in an 'alienated' world, with the distant and often frustrated hope, as George Szirtes wrote in his T.S. Eliot lecture, 'that language and experience are parts of a whole; that … signifier and signified are briefly, triumphantly, consolingly, connected …'

March for the Alternative
(London, 26 March 2011)

As the year turned and the clocks moved forward
we brought rough music to shame the capital:
a spring tide of homespun tribes with pagan
banners and chants congealing the streets, spilling
over the Embankment; ran tan brass stuff
recycled from military detritus
scattered round the world's empires, subverted
into the currency of offbeat streetbands;

a Lenten charivari of dancing girls
with flags on a grey day under
prunus trees, a whiffler with a
bilious Guy Fawkes mask, a skimmity ride
of signs and slogans and awkward curses
with mugshots on placards like spoiled paper money
waving past small change of dandelions, coltsfoot,
scattered by banks of municipal daffodils;
and *Eric Pickles Ate My Youth Club,*
The Associated Society of Engineers
and Firemen – Doncaster Branch, Smile
You're on Police Camera, NO CUTS,
a floating airship of inflated scissors;

and inverted echoes of old market streetcries
from garlanded union reps, physiotherapists,
trainee teachers, assistant librarians,
junior nurses, rappers and samba crews;
a scumbled flood to Hyde Park where a morris side
and a woman with wicker antlers circled
on the field as folk shuffle-streamed by to flex
a free and common right, sympathetic magic,
that the sound of perhaps a million spent feet
might be heard, and the debt to winter deferred.

'SPEEDER CLAIMED CAR WAS DRIVEN BY HER DEAD MOTHER'
(found headline in *Metro* free newspaper)

I went down thinking I'd spent too long folded up
Shrinking from the grasp of the sun, other things.

All my life I'd sidled into rooms, stuttered back
Braking with my heels.   I came through

just a faint opacity, no more than a slight film
on your skin, to help you my girl to do as I

should have done: open up, foot down, make the sun run.

Message from an agnostic angel

I've learned how to lie but I'm still with you,
still aboard our ship with ribs of stone carved
to look like whales' jawbones or boles of oak
edged with arrow heads, dragons' teeth. We sail upside
down and miles inland, propelled by the sound of cellos
lyrical in the rising wind. Shadows of branches quiver
on the stained glass (by the way, they never
got the wings right). The bow of this Romanesque ark
points east, as though it knows where it's going.

Yes, we're concert stowaways in the crescent-
vaulted space, heathen and spooked by the visceral
thrill of unbelief, waywardness, and it's too late
or early for the arches' suffused light
to be the sun. The music's transcendent, still.

Wiggy in Cornwall

He had a thick black forelock
above his brown eyes:
she called him 'Wiggy'. He'd gone bald
long before I was conceived
in Lamorna – but on our childhood
holidays in Praa Sands or Polzeath
he still emerged from the sea
tossing back his missing fringe,
as water streamed from his brow, face,
moustache, the hairs on his chest.

My father always loved seals
I remembered yesterday, more
than fifty years after those '50s
annual bleached transparencies –
we watched them, the seals, off Kelsey Head,
past Porth Joke: the adults inert,
speckled and fecund, draped on rocks;
their young whooshing through waves
like spermatozoa
with a luminous slipstream, and
convulsing back up the slope.

And back in Crantock, by the
dunes close to the Gannel,
protean, he came in
on the tide of last night's dream.

Banner for Bid

The heron we displaced from his grey pool near the hospice
described a ragged parabola, a vowel from a lost
alphabet, away then up to a high branch where he sulked
like a hunched old man, recalibrating his angled gaze,
a heraldic silhouette in argent light and frost.

You are marooned inside this still and quiet place
surrounded by dazzling flotsam: fabric, photos,
flowers, drifts of memorabilia – you the traveller,
founder of weaving workshops in Nepal, lifeline
for refugees, culture explorer, art teacher.

You live now in the blink of the moment:
words, places, and the last ten minutes here
just dissolve. Through the window you watch
the birds swoop down to seed heads, stitching
and unstitching the pale, hazy air.

You say that you see your whole landscape
being slowly rubbed out. A head cut
out, 'erased' in heraldry, is jagged-
edged, floats free. You're still
curious, becalmed but

emblazoned in this flat
perspective as lines
converge to vanishing
point on the near
horizon.

Hyperlinks in Mesopotamia, Oxford

we pace the path between two streams where
the Cherwell forks thinking of causeways
and Portland the earliest grave there
bearing my name oddly spelt like
my great-grandfathers' who chiselled stone and fished
and felt the pebbled arc of Chesil Beach
a rough bulwark to mainland and kimberlins
the lovely tombolo sculpted by accident
umbilical too this ancestral tie

beyond Land's End westward just off St Agnes but
joined at low tide a submarine mooring
lonely and other there lies the Gugh
pagan it needed no mist or mythology
magnification of barrows and dolmens
from there we really saw sunset and moonrise
simultaneously bisecting the sea
spinning the planet spearing the cloudsurf
thrilling lines cast to catch fast-forward shoals

my father-in-law died on Leap-Year-Day
Hugh had an oblique sly sense of humour
and a powerful steer on the straight and the true
our hyphenated relationship was
(of course) accidental reserved and unspoken
but I loved him a brain's neurones
may pulse and leap across the synapses
by choice conjuring remembrance
at least in the skull and its depthless black mirror

Morning in Chapultepec

On a wide pavement that's not sinking
back into the old Aztec lake
there's a wave of five workmen sweeping:
synchronised votives in a ritual dance.

Each different coloured broom-head is too
loud: red, orange, neon pink, acid green,
and a shimmering jacaranda blue.
The dust rolls on, plumes of it gleam.

Their soft arcs massage the stone slabs
in syncopation, a canon
beneath their backchat and stabs
of laughter. Fruit still addles

the air from last night's stalls – pedestrian
hazards festooned with bulbs like tapers
glowing over shrines or the ribbons,
icons, and crosses on baroque altars.

On the road from here, in the low morning sun
a sliver of all the signal spectrum,
a pulse of light parcels, unveils the plain:
volcanoes and outcrops singe the horizon.

And the feathered serpent brought down from the stars,
his fiery plumage Orion's belt.
We made glyphs bright with cinnabar, the colour
of blood, smoking like snakes' tongues.

The sound ladder

In our language we have one word only
for breath, sigh, whisper, and gasp,
but six for different clicks of the tongue.

We refresh our souls by chanting
in the otherguess light before dawn
while we dress for the annual reunion.

Here we make black kites from silk
shed in spring by giant stag beetles –
their old carapaces the size of doors:

stretched on frames they become dry
drums for the wind to call our ancestors
who rise up the sound ladder against a sky

bright as a new painted guiro.
On our mountain, in our cool hall
on firework night we hear ice music:

our marimba a frozen waterfall,
ice rings out in thin fluorescent air,
a catch, a loop of lunar noise.

The instruments are melting, slippery,
and hearing the light, our shaman, scruffy
in moth-eaten fur, bells, feathers,

barks through his ice-horn: sound
waves reverberate in space, spread, curl out
to protect the far edges of this world.

Flags in East Dulwich
(1918–1938)

The autumn air was festooned with bells and all
the houses put out flags, like exhaled breath
for Armistice. Just seven, she remembered
the folded Union Jack in the attic:
as she unfurled its dust her mother
snatched the cloth – 'We've nothing,
nothing to celebrate.' The letter
from Salonica lay still on the table.

Twenty years later in spring, the rules
for the flat were no pets or children:
the dog and cat were installed, then twins.
Looking up to the guttural canoodling of doves,
brisk and undaunted by threats of another war,
she'd hang out the bright forbidden washing.

Resurrection

The medium is magical: a mesh mould lifted
old clothes, sails and rope fibres, an organic jumble
sinewed with chain and laid lines, then coated
with glue from boiled bones, to make off-white paper
that will take ink tannins. It's a strong enough sizing
to carry still the marks from a dead bird's feather
– a mortuary block and a figure half-rising,
Mantegna's unnerving 'Man on a Stone Slab':

Lazarus perhaps, waking from a dead sleep, his bulk
borne on his left arm; his sheet's ridges form
a foreshortened panorama. Gazing
amongst ghosts of pages and a crowd's awkward shuffle
for perspective in the museum's old Reading Room,
I feel my foot, as though willing a high-jump, lifting.

Milvus Milvus

The mates' call and response plays
across a stretch of space between
two sets of jostling spars.

The eyes beneath the kites' wings
tilt, gaze at the horizon's dazzle,
compass the landscape's circumference,

and chart currents that skim a portolan map:
no hinterland, just an annotated
buff shoreline and limitless washes of blue.

Set to their reedy bosun's pipe the birds'
forked rudders and russet stunsails tack,
reach, luff, and plunder through

the clear light's drag and push into
all the dimensions of the streaming air.

EMILY BALLOU is an Australian poet, novelist and screenwriter. Her first collection, *The Darwin Poems* (2009), was published by the University of Western Australia Press. It was awarded the 2010 Wesley Michel Wright Poetry Prize, and was shortlisted for a number of awards. She recently adapted two episodes of the award-winning mini-series *The Slap*. She lives in Glasgow.

'The Importance of Tea' was first published in *Meanjin* (72: 2), edited by Judith Beveridge. 'Twenty-three pictures of the desert' formed a part of the exhibition catalogue for *Shaun Gladwell: Stereo Sequences* (Australian Centre for the Moving Image, June 2011).

These three poems (or these 26 short sequences) came about as a result of being asked to contribute 'some of your words' for an exhibition catalogue on the work of Australian visual artist Shaun Gladwell. Shaun's work captures a series of performances within Australian landscapes, particularly the Australian desert around Broken Hill, NSW. Having been transplanted, as it were, to Scotland, after twenty years of living and writing under Australia's sun, this request allowed me to revisit, reinhabit and to inscribe my longing for those red landscapes and that country. During my early 'explorations', the character of Lizard – outlaw, *flâneur*, performance artist – was born, and he was later discovered (as if by excavation) amongst the journals that the nineteenth-century German explorer Ludwig Leichhardt kept during his own mapping of those Australian deserts.

Years ago, Shaun and I discussed anonymity in art and lately, I have been more and more drawn to writing poetry that plays with the concept of anonymity, to finding better ways to take myself out of the poems, excavating them from another source than myself. Writing through 'character' – an extended portrait of Charles Darwin in *The Darwin Poems* – was one way. 'The Importance of Tea', other than a single line, is entirely collated ('collaged' might be the better word) from Leichhardt's own journals. In 'Twenty-three pictures of the desert' I attempted to capture the graffiti of a lizard's tail, one long line, traced in the sand as he passes though the ephemera left by our civilisation at the end of the world. From this longer sequence, a series of Lizard poems was born, guided by that totem figure, the anonymous lizard who has taken to heart Yeats's command: '*Cast a cold Eye / on Life, on Death*'. I like to think that pesky Lizard (who plagued my typewriter and insisted himself into being whether I liked it or not) is like poetry itself: an all-seeing stillness on a rock, then a sudden darting, dashing off a line in the red hot sand.

The Importance of Tea

A pot of tea and a pigeon between us
we continued our course to the north-east.
Brown thought ourselves lost, disheartened and grumbled.
Giving our position every consideration
I determined upon returning
to those mountains where we had last turned and took
a north-west course again.
The country was as wretched as we, and at night
we almost dropped
from our saddles with fatigue. Another pigeon
was divided between us, but our tea was gone.

I swallowed the bones and the feet of the bird
to stop my stomach. A sleeping lizard
with a blunt tail and knobby scales, fell into our hands;
roasted of course and greedily eaten.
Brown lost all courage. *'We are lost, we are lost,'*
was all he could say. All my words and assurances,
all my telling him that we might be starved for a day
or two, but that we should most certainly find
our party again, could not appease him. Like the lizard we'd eaten,
his eyes flickered quickly to catch each impression on his retina
most minute, remarkably exact
trees peculiarly formed or grouped, broken branches
to recognise again, where we were and where we had been.

This poem was assembled from Ludwig Leichhardt's *Journal of an Overland Expedition in Australia*, chapter 4; 18 January 1845.

Twenty-three pictures of the desert

1. The prevailing winds brought you here
    in the insect drift from the Pacific;
    you came with wings over the long plateau
    along the denuded hills and cathedrals of rock
    over the gossan spill, wind pressing onward
    carrying gum leaves and soil
    the crushed wreckage of mountains, in its rotor coil, onward
    the red dust

2. Before it was called anything else it had no name,
    it was just place and then it was called Leaping Crest by those
    who saw it first and saw it for a long time. No
    sounds but the wind, no sounds but the driving wind.

3. You wonder for the cities, their car-clogged streets and
                how our days
    were spent packing useless items, or calling friends, and who
    would catalogue the final gestures,
    those first abandoned, those kept longest, clutched,
    until the very end.

4. And who would be the archivist of last things.

5. Who would make a catalogue of exhalations, the photos
                taken
    when the shutter was closed, drawers of leaves shaped
                like hands
    nomenclature of colours collected by night after the sun
                has fallen.
    Would we leave our closets full of missed human shrugs
                and sighs?
    Would every empty house speak emptily of goodbyes and
                last traces?

6.   Here, the road was always just a long red sigh
a jagged line scraped in the dirt with a stick
that would turn to mud if the clouds ever came
and when they do now they fatten and taunt the claypan
the saltbush the bluebush and the grasses of the slopes
with lightning and rising thirst. They form and move and
        fall and disperse
as they always have, according to their own cloud rules
        and physics.

7.   The bird calls at dawn
are the loudest songs
(the breaking of leaf and seed in beak,
the tree-shaken scramble for branches)
the world will make all day.
The only shadows are those the birds throw down
and the long stretched stains, twice their height
of roos straining forward, ricocheting off red earth
in elastic band propulsion, the pogo mob
the boundary riders
contracting and leaping away from falling light.

8.   Will the archivist know the difference between a wave that
        beckons and one
that departs, and also, that takes its leave for the very last
        time
does anybody have a picture of that? And where would
        you find it?
Who will keep track of the raptures of three a.m.
who will keep the marks where paws once pressed against
        wet concrete
who will say again, let's meet for coffee at two, at that café
with tables on the street, where the people pass with
        loaves of bread
and greet each other and the glossy cars glide by in search
        of parking spaces.
Who will keep the artefacts of the streets? The hats with
        brass coins in them
the tramp's trolley with the broken wheels, the faces of lost
        cats pasted to poles.

And all the casual glances passed between strangers, has
    somebody
made a record of that? And will you drop the stylus so we
    can listen to the sound?

9.   The sun is a scorched immensity
it etches then sleeps
the wind keeps the cool of the blue gums;
how the pale light once fell
with the dust of wattle flowers
and left your skin warmer than childhood.
You could take the loveliness of a place
for granted; you could rub away the bark to the smooth
    red trunk beneath
catch the clots of sticky gum on your thumbs
collect the upturned curls of grey-green leaves
sage smiles unleashed and crack their stems and seams
for the heady fumes, the blue oil you will never smell again.
It always was a country of fire. It still is
though nobody tends the boundaries or marks it on a map
    when it comes
and nobody knows anymore what it takes.
Houses that smoulder without tears. Eucalyptus manna
    that still pours
from a hole in the bark of the white gum, holds the colour
    of fire
and gathers like paper snakes on the ground
waiting to burn.

10.   Here are all the paper lamps, moon-shaped, that swayed
    from our ceilings
imprinted, tin-plated, with golden light.
We each had a sun in our room to remind us we were just
    a planet
that hovered and hung somewhere in vast night and for a
    short time.
Here are the shapes of lit windows, and the shapes that
    passed within them
and passing trains, each small square stretched
into a string of light and a *chi chi, chi chi*

shuddering over the tracks. *When using the telegraph*
twenty-three means break the line.
Machines and lamps mean nothing now.
They are dumb and still; they are carcass.

11.   And here is a Polaroid of the desert from sky to floor
        told as shade, spoken
        as the tint of things that might have stayed:
        Pewter Grey: silver-pink inner ears
        of a young red kangaroo / slab of chalky lime
        stone / the ash-grey spots of a Leopardwood tree.
        Stonewashed Denim: a lizard's pointed tongue / the veins
        of desert opal / the clustered petals
        of a Blue Pincushion.
        Watermelon: the stem of a Coolabah leaf / pink
        throat of Shingleback / Rhodonite crystals.
        Sun Yellow: flower of Prickly Wattle / the mouth of a Jacky
                Dragon / pyromorphite.
        Bright Idea: iris of an emu eye / gold sand / the stripes
        of a Rock-wallaby's tail.
        Banner Red: curled furred shavings of mulga tree
                bark / Spessartine garnets
        the beak of a lorikeet.
        Hosta Leaf: sage foliage of a Desert Pea / wing of King Parrot
        the banded masses of malachite.

12.   Did you ever paint a car those colours?
        Did you drive it cross-country and disappear? A desert twin.
        You could pass within. You could inhabit it, provisional,
                momentary.
        Though you would never have it. It would never be you
        or yours, they said. And told you often. You are no
                resident of the red places.
        Show me the dust on your hands, what colour is it?
        No, no, you are not from here. See the olive tinge to your
                skin
        the European traces.
        Open your mouth and speak, what sound is it?
        Your vowels are strange and twisted as ragged tree-roots
        your consonants bulge from the ground, searching a hold

and a drink, with obvious transplantation.
Do your ears turn, marsupially, with the wind? Do they
        tune in?
Your dog was more dingo than you. Your dog was more
        red. She's the true citizen
of the sun. There's no gate you can cross to get in
to this rusted heart any longer. Your memories are fugue
        states
dusty water holes where no water has been
for a decade. Keep looking,
keeping looking in, although you're elsewhere.

13.   And what you learned was this: there's no continental grip
for deserters. We're in slow drift.
Upsidedown. You're 23 skidoo. You're gone.

14.   We came to the Silver City in a dream
then haunted the coal seam
we are just one
of the creatures Extremely Rare and Seldom Seen
that sometimes flit through these parts, moving with thirst
then descend into cooler and darker dens
burrowing into a curve of temporal bone
while the sun and moon come out in their turn.

15.   At night Lizard emerges
to catch the debris the wind has left
his body sweeps clean the plains
the dunefields and the folded eroded slopes
his body draws on sand, unscrolls
an elegant story
told in whorls, the small flowers
of his claws, the long kick of his tail, the waves
I have been, everywhere and nowhere, the same.

16.   Lizard leaves his signature, his graffiti
        " /
             "

    wind erases it.

17.   The archivist of all lost things opens the canister, unspools
                the black strip
    with the edges notched in sprockets. It was made of tree-
                pulp and camphor
    so flammable it burned underwater, one frame could ignite
    entire rooms and reels, whole cinemas, a century of pictures.
    Then came the polyesters, so thick they cracked the
                projectors;
    afterwards, acetate which merely bubbled and melted over
                time.
    But still, you can see, beneath the mechanisms of
                deterioration
    the iron stain, here, under the street-lamp, the hazy, faded
                shape of a dancer
    here, a solitary midnight walker, here
    the soft clanging of sail-boat rigs in the harbour and the
                black bats overhead
    they still fly,
    every night, from tree to sky, over the dark city.

18.   You walked then
    you wanted to be upright
    you carried your own load and your life on your back
    sometimes you wanted the sun to end
    the long road to end or to slow
    or to go on, and it did all these things.

19.   The breath of the sea burns
    through the empty buildings, then blows beyond the
                treeless plains
    it bleaches the scarps
    the crops of lime and dolomite
    and stumbles over the ledges
    catching in caves along the gorges where kestrels still hover;

the rivers once ran here
left such wide soft marks, such dried out memories of
            water, deep claws of rocks
where horses stumbled and stopped. Thirsting. Tasting
            salt. Disappearance.

20.   And you are there, not quite sky and not quite land
       like the wind, invisible, mercurial, visible
       only when the dust is heavy. You are no more
       than sand, and soon less:
       the sketch of a face after the shadow saw it.
       Flickers with some of the frames missing
       a fossil in a margin of light.
       Desert's conflagration. Trees that burn.
       These are merely instances.

21.   Faded due to image oxidation
       faded due to prolonged light exposure
       uneven dye fade
       atmospheric ozone, gelatin yellowing
       heavy stain and silver mirroring
       emulsion delamination
       and cracking
       from contact with sunlight, air and water.

22.   The archivist of lost things' most precious thing
       is a slab of footpath chalked with marks that track
       all the steps taken back and forth on a single day
       a score of human traffic.

       This is the mark that means forward motion with
                   purpose ::::
       This is the sign for shuffle along | |
       This is the mark that stands for darting through crowds
                   when late √
       This is a wave ~
       This a friendly glance passed between strangers ˆ ° ˆ ˇ
       This is standing still chatting while children run
                   around. ≈Δ~

This pause a lonely stillness in the middle of the footpath {i}
This an acceleration towards an old friend «/ \»
Chalked together, the archivist's lost square keeps an
        equation
without beginning or answer, and without end.

23.   And if you could show them, how would you show them.

I, Lizard, performance artist

enact mediative studies
in the physics of gravity
motion vs. stillness
metaphysics, in particular
cyclical time.

My work muses on anonymity
the relation of body to place
the inevitability of decay
being ephemeral
object in space.

My art is my performance.
My performance is endurance.

PAUL BATCHELOR was born in Northumberland. At Newcastle University, he wrote a PhD on Barry MacSweeney's poetry. He now works as a freelance teacher and reviews regularly for the *Guardian* and the *TLS*. His first book, *The Sinking Road*, was published by Bloodaxe in 2008. He has received an Eric Gregory Award, the Arthur Welton award, and the 2009 *Times* Stephen Spender Prize for Translation; he also won the 2009 Edwin Morgan International Poetry Competition. www.paulbatchelor.co.uk.

Coal has always been synonymous with the exploitation of both the working class and the environment. Given the fact that my father, both of my uncles and both grandfathers were miners of one sort or another, and that I grew up in the 1980s, when the mining industry was destroyed, it should have been possible for me to write a poem of straightforward solidarity or condemnation on the matter. 'Brother Coal' is not that poem. Instead, something more ambiguous emerged, and the poem is as much about coming to poetry as anything else. Perhaps it is simply impossible to express an undivided loyalty in poetry. Poetry wants all of the loyalty for itself. In his essay on *Coriolanus*, William Hazlitt stated this in stark, unforgettable terms: 'The language of poetry naturally falls in with the language of power... Poetry is right royal.'

Similarly, 'Pit Ponies' did not turn out as I had intended. I wanted to write about the strike of 1984–85, but found myself focusing on a much smaller strike in the 1940s. Pit ponies would usually be stabled underground, and only brought up when the pit shut down for its annual holiday, or for a strike. 'Pit Ponies' likens the excitement the ponies displayed on such occasions to the hopes of the striking miners. The poem was written in response to an account I heard of the ponies being brought up; and also to Wilfrid Gibson's poem 'The Ponies', which describes a similar event, and includes some nice touches, before ending somewhat desperately with the lines: 'Mayhap one day / Our masters, too, will go on strike, and we / Escape the dark and drudgery of the pit, / And race unreined around the fields of heaven!'

Like many of my recent poems, 'Brother Coal' and 'Pit Ponies' took a long time to write: three and five years respectively. My fascination with Rilke's French poems arose at a time when I worried that this slow-burn work might permanently cut me off from the impulse to write lyric poems. Rilke's French poems are brief, beautiful, intense, odd, fragile things, and I hoped that translating them might keep that line of communication open.

Brother Coal

I

Childhood fantasies, the kind that die hard,
staged in the darkness of the coal shed;
a mother's boy knuckling down for a shift
of glamorous, imaginary graft;
the difficult one, ideas below his station,
a could-be diamond lacking in ambition –
and there you are as always, there you are,
playmate, shadow, secret sharer,
genius loci of the bunker, fast asleep
like a tramp wrapped tight in a dirty oil-cape.

II

From back-to-backs that echo with raised voices
to row against row of little, Dutch-style houses;
the rec, the tip, the cornershop, the street,
a warren of cul-de-sacs, my earthly estate –
except I never liked to play outside.
Scholarly, timid, anxious to succeed,
first chance I got I left it all behind
and then (I couldn't help myself) returned.
Sooner than I would dare admit I sensed
that this is all I stay buoyed up against.

III

My childish heart sinks like a falling flare.
Dad asks if he is making himself clear:
No pets allowed. In this house all the warmth
we can afford is right there in the hearth,
where you cringe on your haunches in the cree
or spatter awake in wet coughs and outcry.
You drowse open-eyed. You settle and resettle
as a dog curled in its basket might shift a little,
lift its muzzle to salute a ghost
and then – sigh of the disregarded – resume its rest...

IV

A black cabinet painted shut, the spellbound doors
promising untold tinctures and liqueurs –
a miser's hoard, a treasure trove cool to the touch,
though never as cold as the spent white ash
he had to rake out last thing every night
(he too was cold, he too was spent and white).
I see him on his knees as though in prayer,
huffing and puffing life into the fire;
I see him rise, the cupped flare of a match
like sudden anger. He too was quick to catch.

V

Fibred, veined, fissured like an icicle –
black, pleated muscle ripped with black blood-crystal.
It stranged my mind that I could never lift
a shovelful or lug a sack – the heft!
So much unmanageable worldliness
overmatching me! – and yet a single piece
felt buoyant, quick and subtle, easily borne.
Before such mysteries, I hunker down
in contemplation. I turn and burn
in claustral darkness. I found a church of one.

VI

Implicit as the fault in a flawed prism
or the seamless ambiguity of a poem,
your darker promise: to give nothing away.
To make us pay for everything. To someday
run out on us, that we might balance the cost
of losing you against all that was lost
when you were found, hung in your galleries,
entombed within yourself, far from the sun's rays –
a fluted curtain no wind stirs;
sails of wet leather, a black ship in black waters…

VII

Compacted sentiment, this pseudo-factual,
homely, far-fetched stuff. O, Brother Coal,
shine your black torch on such complacency
for shame! Shine your black torch that I may see
each brush-off, cave-in and betrayal
implicated in your comet's tail.
O, stardust of disasters and diseases,
child labour, roof collapse and silicosis,
let me stand face to face with your dark mirror
until the shadows glitter and grow clear.

Pit Ponies
But what is that clinking in the darkness?

Louis MacNeice

Listen. They're singing in your other life:
'Faith of our Fathers' sounding clear as day
from the pit-head where half the village has turned out
to hear the latest news from underground,
news that will be brought to them by the caged ponies
hauled up and loosed in Raff Smith's field.

Could that have been you in Raff Smith's field,
mouthing the words and listening to the cages lift,
watching sunlight break on dirty ponies,
noting the way, unshoed for their big day,
each one flinches on the treacherous ground,
pauses and sniffs, then rears and blunders about?

As at a starting pistol they gallop out
and a roll of thunder takes hold of the field –
thunder, or else an endless round
of cannon fire. Hooves plunge and lift.
They pitch themselves headlong into the day:
runty, fabulously stubborn pit ponies.

But they seem to have a sense, the ponies,
a sidelong kind of sense about
getting called in at last light on the fifth day:
they seem to know the strike has failed,
as though they felt the tug of their old lives.
They shake their heads. They shy and paw the ground.

Let's leave them there for now, holding their ground
for all it's worth, and say the ponies
might maintain their stand-off, as the livid
shades of miners might yet stagger out
of history into the pitched field
dotted with cannonballs you see today.

Let's pretend you might come back some day
to wait a lifetime on this scrap of ground
until the silence – like the silence of a field
after a battle – breaks, and you hear ponies
buck and whinny as the chains pay out
and once again the rusty cages lift…

As though the day was won, as though the ground
was given, the ponies gallop out
to claim their piece of field, their only life.

from *The Orchards*
after Rilke

I

My heart could wake the tongues of angels
and make them sing their memories –
but the voice I raise
belongs to someone else.

Silence draws it out,
never to return –
so tender, so brazen –
who knows what will become of it?

II

Night light, secret sharer,
even if we lose ourselves you won't reveal
my heart. The south side of this hill
glows with a sunset aura

but you shine on, burning for the student,
longing to interrupt his study:
just once to disturb somebody
so they look up and see you: that's all you want.

(And such simplicity uproots an angel.)

III

Rest easy should you find
an angel at your table: these things happen.
Make sure the wine is open,
smooth the tablecloth, and never mind

that our food must seem gross
to so refined a palate. Let him eat.
Let him raise a humble glass
to those exquisite lips. He will be glad of it.

IV

How often have we spoken to the flowers
in confidence
as though they were the balance
in which we'd take the measure of our passion?

In the dark hours –
when the strongest cannot hold us up, when
the weakest cannot hold us down –
when the stars dance in confusion

then we are free.
For then nothing supports us but
the table and the bed:
the bed the table hopes someday to be.

V

Everything happens – slowly at first,
as though someone accused
the apple of being good to eat,
tempting us to let it rot

or grow until the bough breaks;
tempting us to have it cast
in bronze; or this – the last, the worst –:
to wish that it were made of wax.

VI

Who can say how ruled we are
by what the Invisible turns back?
The unseen life gives way before
the unseen trick.

So, according to our desires, our centre shifts –
and the heart, free of its gifts,
free of its inheritance,
declares itself Grand Master of Absence.

VII   Palm

Palm. Soft, unmade bed.
Crumpled blankets left
when the dreaming stars awoke and rose
to the skies.

Having slept here,
are they rested?
Burning, clear,

back in their endless round
among their kind…

Cold, bereft,
the bed of my hand
feels weightless, having let go those
blazoned stars.

VIII

A man's all-but-final word may be
a cry of misery,
but witnessed by his conscience, as by his mother,
his final word will be beautiful.

In the end we must gather
into ourselves the whole of desire; must speak
a word so bountiful
no bitterness can hope to hold it back.

IX

Sing a god
and he will answer you with silence.
None of us advance
except towards a silent god.

But we never see the deal we've struck.
Empty-handed, shivering –
we never see the trick
by which the angels inherit everything.

X

The Centaur is so wise
to overleap the seasons of our world –
our new-born world: a promise
only he can make good –

and there Hermaphrodite stands: unequalled,
sheltered, perfect.
Who does not wish to find the lost half of a demi-god?
Where haven't we looked?

XI   Cornucopia

Somewhere your opening
calyx turns to catch the sun
and you offer yourself like a blessing.
We wait for you, beautiful horn!

Blossom... Blossom... Blossom
making a bed as it falls
for fruit that is already ripening...
Lift an apple: feel the curves pulse.

How the world rushes
to attack us when we fail –
how it punishes
our hearts for being already full.

Through you the miracle is given,
O horn of excess, O hunting
horn resounding
with the breath of heaven.

XII

As Murano glass
will remember
the cloud-grey glare
in which it forms as bliss,

your tender hands
know from a dream
they are the slow balance
that fills our moments to the brim.

CHRISTY DUCKER lives in Northumberland. Her pamphlet *Armour* (Smith/Doorstop, 2011) was a Poetry Book Society Choice, and is also a Read Regional title for 2012–13. Her poetry commissions include residencies for Port of Tyne and English Heritage. Some of her recent work appears in the collaborative book *Tyne View* (New Writing North, 2012). She has received the Andrew Waterhouse Prize, and is currently writing a series of poems about Grace Darling, as part of her PhD research at Newcastle University.

These poems address the hidden history of Grace Darling, a nineteenth-century lighthouse-keeper. Overnight, Darling became famous for saving nine lives at sea. The subsequent attention made her ill and she died at the age of twenty-six. Beyond these basic facts, silence. Or so I thought.

Some years ago, I began to read the Darling archive. Her letters challenged the heroic myth, and detailed a strange reality. I was struck by the extremes of her life, how literate she was, how scientifically expert. She broke the mould in ways that went unnoticed, ways I wanted to salvage in poems.

'Grace Darling's ABC' is an abecedary sequence. Eight of the twenty-six poems are included here. Although alphabetical, the sequence is not chronological. There is one poem for every year of Darling's life – each links an experience to a letter shape. In Darling's notebooks, she decorates her letters and gives them different attributes. I wanted this to inform my poems, and show how Darling inhabited her own literacy.

There are three further poems here. These introduce 'Grace Darling's Journal', a ten-poem sequence about reluctant fame. The 'Journal' shows Darling besieged by fans, her island wrecked by their clamour for souvenirs. As the sequence progresses, lines grow longer, rhyme more insistent, and Darling's loss of privacy more pronounced.

Together, these poems explore the cross-currents that make a life. My aim is a humanist biography of Darling, alert to her public and private stories. I feel poetry and biography sit well together, as poems and lives are each sustained by breath.

from *Grace Darling's ABC*

A

is the point of intention
she sees at the tip of her pen,
when guiding it over paper
to carve out her ABCs,

starting with A's composure,
its gable and its crossbeam
strong enough to house ideas
and hold a family of noises

various as the baby's *clack*,
her father's Sunday yawn
or, less pronounced, that bit of throat
she sounds before a song begins.

B

is the plump consolation
her father brings back from war,
when teaching her B is for *Bouche*
or *Bacioni* not just bairn –

a letter she fattens with ink
and practice, to bolster him
up from his memories. She writes it
as two kissy-lips beginning

to spell out *Brownsman*, her home
a roost of birds and books
where daughters can grow like sons,
embracing the broad horizons.

C

is the widemouth, hag-back, tongueless
retch of a letter on her lips
in the room where she dies, all *cough*
from her cobweb lungs, a threat

since childhood, when C would sigh
in the nest of her name yet croak
like a corvid without. Too hard
to prettify, as is what lies

beyond herself in her dying
on eider, when C marshals clot
and contortion, a life consumed
too soon, the slew of condolence.

I

is the seedling she grows
from a compost of guillemot shit
and stones, her tiny conductor
of life between air and soil,

outstretched as her way of saying *aye*
to every chance of garden
that holds its own against the salt
where she sprouts up through childhood,

finding I is how she writes
herself on the page as a stalk
with a knuckled root, a plumb back,
a bud at the head unfurling.

O

is that look of admiration
cast towards her fame's gold sun,
it's what makes her a hero,
the medal they pin to her front

quite something, yet also nothing,
O is the shape of a secret,
the coins she earns from salvage
locked in a drawer but haunting her,

all lined up as if to score
a requiem of silver Os,
flat as the faces of drowned men
she pulls from the sea like moons.

T

is neater than how she feels,
when reading Thomasin's name
in winter, seeing the T as bold –
a mast above the storm.

Its square shoulders, its level best
are what she tries to emulate
whenever hurricanes coop her in
and bend the Longstone sideways.

Her letters fold their wings and wait
to flock to her sister in spring,
dreaming of mainland treetops
while perched at the tip of her tongue.

W

is a sudden wave
that swells inside her body,
gathering pace before it crests
as breasts that seem half skin, half sea

each time they fatten with the moon
or pool back in her armpits;
two points to be skimmed over
by tailoring and family talk

of *woman, wife, due warning*: words
that throw their arms up at her shape,
as halfway through her life she learns
her flesh now has an undertow.

Z

is a burst of Congolese
in the Bamburgh Castle library,
the day a *Zebra* springs at her
from page ninety-eight of Bewick –

a zigzag into the new
so rare, it dazzles her eyes
with its lightning bolt, auguring
times that will happen without her

when zoos will open and dizzy up,
the zoetrope spin her tale,
and words sprint on to catch the sense
of modernity's *zip* and *zooming* –

from *Grace Darling's Journal*

1838 –
Sepr. 10

The drowned are gone,
the live ones still
fill every room
with their lumber –

grief, wet wool
and gratitude.
One never speaks,
might not again

though each wound talks
incessantly.
Sometimes, I lie
on a table

at night, to sleep
above their sea
of sheets. I dream
their cries are birds.

Sepr. 11

A flotilla arrives
with barrels of bacon,
oats and barley, wanting
answers, survivors, proof

the rumour's based on truth.
There's Smeddle, brandishing
papers and promises
I will have a silk dress;

poor father grappling
press men with clarty shoes
to land, and Lloyds are here
of course, in raven coats

to check on each last thing.
The living have eaten
October already
and I must feed us all.

Sepr. 15

From Scotland, a letter that bursts
its praise around the room like mess
I could do without – a big fesh
about nowt, as father would say –

the Lady who writes has visions
of me in my boat, collisions
of monstrous waves and my valour
rising above the swell, no doubt

she's read a number of novels –
why else would she think I'd 'loose locks
flowing in storm force winds', or ask
for a snip of my humdrum hair,

the same I had in rags that night,
the same which starts to hackle now
I have to answer these strangers
who wheedle away at sorrow.

LYNN JENNER's book *Dear Sweet Harry* (Auckland University Press, 2010) won the New Zealand Society of Authors Prize for Best First Book of Poetry in 2010. *Dear Sweet Harry* is a mixed-genre work, telling stories of Harry Houdini, Mata Hari and the author's own grandfather, Harry. Lynn is a PhD student at the International Institute of Modern Letters in Wellington.

'The Russian Point of View' was published in *Turbine* (2010); 'I have a feeling…' in *Hue and Cry*, 5 (2011); 'The hot early universe' in *Trout*, 17 (2012); 'Six New Zealand Jews…' in *Turbine* (2009).

I often tell stories in my poems. I want the reader to share, by the look and feel of the design, as much as by the words, the way a situation unfolds and meanings constantly change as time passes. My aim is that the real-time experience of reading tells the story of the poem as much as its words do.

My poems often come from my reactions to everyday events, and to what I am reading. 'The Russian Point of View' is a good example of this, beginning with news of the first of the 8000-odd earthquakes to hit Christchurch in September 2010 and showing in its form the process all of us – my mother, me, the journalists, the experts, the cat and the turtle – go through in those first few days, trying to do what is necessary and to make sense of what has happened.

I am also very interested in memory, especially the ways that individuals' memories are made up of collective and social memories as well as things that only happened to them and can be remembered in their own senses. 'Six New Zealand Jews…' is an example of the complexity that comes from mixing up what everyone knows with the particularity of what one woman, the guide, says on a particular day to a particular group of Jewish people from a faraway place.

Sometimes my poems come from my own practice as a researcher. 'Ten rules to guide me…' came from my experiences meeting survivors of the Holocaust, and 'I'm not sure what to call what I have done' from my desire to be active rather than passive in my investigation of another poet's work. I may be an archive-loving nerdy type in real life, but in my imagination I am fearless.

The Russian Point of View

1. At 7.30 am on Saturday morning my mother phones with news of the earthquake. She does not say that she was frightened. She talks about the cat, which is lost, and how cold the house is.

2. I have a new e book reader loaded with a hundred classics. *e reading anywhere, anytime* it says, as it powers up. It looks primitive, like one of those early mobile phones. Why do I always press 'next' before I have read the last three words on the page?

3. Stepan Arkadyevitch Oblonsky has been carrying on an intrigue with the children's governess. Dolly has found out and will not leave her room. What's to be done? What's to be done? he says to himself in despair.

4. Dolly, he believes, is a woman of limited capacity, but he needs her agreement now for the sale of a certain forest on her property. He compares this need with his need for the roguish black eyes of Mlle Roland. For today anyway, his need for Dolly is greater. He may be sued by his tailor. That is how bad things are.

5. Stepan Arkadyevitch remembers the exact minute when he arrived home, happy and good natured from the theatre, with a huge pear in his hand for his wife, and found her in the wrong room, with the letter that revealed everything in her little hand.

6. Soon after I arrive, my mother tells me that the big earthquake roared like a wild animal. I assume a lion. According to the newspaper the roar of an earthquake is the sound made by the fault slipping. It makes this noise with no consciousness or purpose, my mother says.

7. I picture her waking to the roar of a lion. Stopping to put on her dressing gown and slippers and pick up her torch. No lights at the neighbours', no streetlights, no teeth. Broken glass under her feet. The bitter frost.

8. Stepan Arkadyevitch has summoned his sister, Madame Karenina.

9. 'Do you know Vronsky?' he asks his friend Levin over an excellent dinner. 'Fearfully rich, handsome, great connections, an aide de camp, and with all that a very nice, good natured fellow.'

10. But Vronsky treats Kitty badly. He a man of the world, with two fine rows of teeth, and she a virgin in a ball dress.

11. Next day, Vronsky and Oblonsky are at the Moscow railway station to meet the Petersburg train. Vronsky's mother and Oblonsky's sister have met. The hiss of the boiler on distant rails, the rumble of something heavy.

12. Vronsky steps into Anna's carriage. He notices her breasts.

13. Several men run by with panic-stricken faces. A guard is crushed. Perhaps he was drunk? Perhaps he was so muffled up in the bitter frost that he didn't hear the train?

14. Each morning I inspect cracks in the concrete to see if they have grown. I take photographs of these cracks. I follow instructions for water sterilisation and I clean salad vegetables in boiled water. I feel breathless, as if somehow I can't keep up.

15. Bedrock gets loaded up with stress because it is being dragged on from underneath, says a lecturer in Geological Sciences. It's beautiful, says one of his post-graduate students, one side insisting on change, the other resisting. Change prevailing.

16. Oh no!!! It's Vronsky!!! I text a friend who knows the Russians. He doesn't answer.

17. Please don't fall in love with Vronsky, I say to Karenina, but I know she will.

18. The first duty of the duty seismologist is to offer
reassurance. The more faults we find that have slipped,
the better, he says. Strain on all the region's faults has
been reduced. Etc. Sometimes the cracking can be
a new fracture, but mostly, and always in large quakes,
the ground gives along existing fault lines.

19. I meet a woman who keeps a turtle. On the night of
the quake she found the turtle, wrapped him in a towel
and held him on her lap. When daylight came, she saw
that he was bleeding from a long cut on his neck.
How strange, she says, that a sharp piece of glass found
the only soft part.

20. A feature writer tells us she cried in the newsroom.
The earthquake has fractured her real estate deal,
leaving her in a landscape which no one had ever seen
before. The most unfeeling of her colleagues asked her
if she was all right.

21. The most unfeeling colleague of the feature writer
who cried in the newsroom has his own column. He is
not afraid at night. He goes with the flow. After all,
there's nothing that he can do to stop it.

22. Anna Karenina will be cut in half by a train. I know
she will.

23. The feature writer who cried in the newsroom writes
that she is not afraid of dying. She is afraid she will not
be able to manage the repayments on five hundred
thousand dollars at the current floating rate.

  • The trend of falling newspaper readership
  among the young continues.
  • The next edition of the Oxford English
  Dictionary may not be published in book form.

24. Experts have come from many places to see the
earthquake. Immediately there is conflict.
The Australian geologists think the fault slipped
east to west, like migration. The Kiwis think

west to east, like the prevailing wind. The Americans
think the break happened at the thin part in the middle.

25. There's the excitement of the fault itself, but then I
talk to people who were affected and it's very sad,
says a scientist for whom English is a third language.

26. Tolstoy helps. 'The answer which life gives to all
questions is: one must live in the needs of the day.'
I wonder if his flat tone, which I savour as a form of
wisdom quite separate from his words, is an artefact
of translation.

27. My bed floats like a dinghy in the turning tide.
After three days the cat returns. Takes up residence
behind the television but comes out at night to sit
at the window, staring in the direction of the fault.

28. You can almost give these things a personality,
says the man who was duty seismologist on a night with
twelve aftershocks. It sometimes feels like they're out to get you.

29. Hyacinths. My mother's brother died when he was
thirteen. Hyacinths in the hospital.

30. Hyacinths on the kitchen windowsill.

31. According to the newspaper, there are two
energy waves. The P wave is fast and travels through
crustal rock. The S wave arrives later. It cannot pass
through liquid or penetrate the earth's outer core.

32. Sometimes there is no warning sound. The nature of
earthquakes allows for this.

33. Two days after I left, my mother tells me that she sat
down in her armchair, thinking to do the crossword, and
found herself crying. Unable to stop.

I have a feeling with no name

It takes the form of nostalgia for understatement,
minimalism, suspicion of artifice or decoration;
nostalgia even for the despotism of this.

It takes the form of sorrow and longing
for the gut floor, the killing chain and the repetition
in the soul of a man who made the same three cuts,
two up and one down,
every minute for eight hours,
with two fifteen-minute breaks and half an hour
for lunch.

It takes the form of tenderness,
for the way the past piles up
into a few notable pinnacles –

A young couple on their wedding day.
A baby in a pram, always in summer,
a woman and a man standing side by side
outside a brick house, she
holds a toddler in her arms.

Children looking into the sun, knee-deep
in a lake or a river or the sea, a car
parked beside a tree, a picnic blanket,
then another young couple on their wedding day,
this time in colour.

A crowd of us
in a small town church,
three times in a single winter.

For Maisie Brown

They fill the church, those women in the red woollen
capes. Brownie had no children, they say, but instead
was mother to a hundred stumbling girls. They speak
of the yellow light which burned at night in the upstairs
window of her flat. How she counted them in as they ran
to beat the clock, kisses tingling on their lips. How she
seemed to know everything from a particular squeal or a
whisper, or the way a girl's shoes squeaked on the lino in
the hall. I was only seventeen when my mother died, one
woman says. I didn't know what to do.

> Everything is softening, falling towards the earth
> Everything is softening, falling towards the earth

They speak of her work. On her morning rounds,
they say, she visited every patient. She might tell a child
with a broken arm not to make such a fuss. But
all Sunday afternoon she would do exercises on the floor
with the polio children. She might tell a dying woman
not to worry, but later she would come back and talk
about how her husband would manage the children.
In those days, they say, with an exchange of glances,
and an odd rising inflection, we had our own eighty-bed
hospital with full surgical facilities. Now of course,
all that is gone.

> Everything is cracking at the edges,
> tearing on the folds

Near the end, the women made themselves a roster.
Every morning at eight, one of them would be there
to rub her heels with oil and wash her face and hands
with scented soap. In the afternoon, another would read
her gossip from the *New Zealand Woman's Weekly*.
Nurse Delaney, Brownie said one day, after seeming
to be asleep for a long time, you have a laugh like a
hyena. Sometimes one of the women would just sit and
hold her hand, while the sun set.

Everything is softening, falling towards the earth
Everything is softening, falling towards the earth

After carefully thanking all who had cared for Brownie,
the women in the red capes leave the church. Outside it
is too hot for capes, so they fold them away in a box
which belongs to the Stratford Hospital Museum.
The capes are different shades of red. Some have
uneven hems. But when she puts the cape around her
shoulders, and buttons the tab across the neck,
each woman feels as if she is her best and truest self.

The hot early universe

Say a person who is male, a certain age, from a certain family,
with a certain body type and state of health, a certain history of
loving and being loved, of wanting to be loved, of being cared
for and abandoned ... say this man, who does certain types of
exercise, has certain religious and spiritual beliefs, works at a
particular job, earns a certain amount which covers, partly covers
or doesn't cover his expenses, which are in a certain pattern
relating to his sources of pleasure ... say he meets a woman ...

Naturally your life reveals itself to her and hers to you ... you
think she is beautiful and she is kind and gentle to you.

Phase equilibrium

You enjoy having a drink with her after work, it reminds you of
your parents, the way things start so quietly when you are tired
after work and so keen to relax, and then there are times with
lots of laughs and good music and you enjoy having a drink with
her.

Solid phase

It reminds you of your parents, the way things start so quietly
when you are tired after work, and then there are times with lots
of laughs and good music, and then about 9 or 10 you want to eat

dinner and she says she doesn't feel hungry, so you cook and she stands around watching, telling you she could do it all better, and when it is ready you dish her some, but mostly she doesn't eat it.

Pressure

And then she is mean and nothing pleases her. Or she laughs and drinks some more and you hear her being sick.

The presence of line-like excitations such as defect lines

But you still think she is beautiful when she is sober and cleaned up. She is often very sweet and gentle to you and only nasty for a couple of hours at night, and she always apologises the next morning, and anyway it reminds you of your parents.

Things start so quietly when you are tired after work, and there are times with lots of laughs and it seems as though this will be a nice night, but then a fight starts and sometimes you get angry at her and swear at her and maybe you leave the house for a walk or maybe you don't.

Water does not instantly turn into gas, but forms a turbulent mixture.

She drinks anything at this time, rummages round in the cupboards for any half bottle of something she didn't drink the night before, and you are tired but too scared to go to bed and leave her raging round the flat, falling against walls, sometimes breaking dishes and glasses and cutting herself.

One day you come home from work and she is on the couch, unconscious.

At the phase transition point the two phases of a substance have identical free energies and therefore are equally likely to exist.

You call the ambulance. You clean the place up and go.

Ten rules to guide me in my research

1. I will not phone deaf old ladies out of the blue. I will arrange to be vouched for, and introduced.
2. I will not bang on people's front doors with my fist, or any metaphorical version of that.
3. I will try to recognise Yiddish words.
4. I will answer questions about my parents, my marital status, my children and their incomes, without flinching.
5. I will make sure I always have a clean hanky.
6. I will try to say German words correctly.
7. *Schpielberg* is the correct pronunciation of the name of the movie director.
8. I will not interrupt old people when they are telling me their story, except if there is a fire alarm.
9. I will not cry unless they do.
10. If they are women, they were beautiful when they were young.

*

After I find a book with the title *This Crazy Thing a Life* I add Rule Eleven: *Life* is Crazy. People are getting by.

*

Much later, having noticed the contributions made by Billy Pilgrim, the Tralfamadorians, Jacques Austerlitz and a man called Bloomfield, from Melbourne, I add two more rules, these to be applied *ex post facto.*

12. It is important to find out things but even more important to avoid harming natural people.
13. Fictional people do not look you in the eye or feel pain. They are available without appointment, and at very little expense. Furthermore, their wellbeing is not a concern to any official bodies. They therefore make excellent research participants, and will be considered whenever possible as a preferable alternative to natural people or the natural descendants of dead people.

Six New Zealand Jews Share Their Impressions
of Oświęcim

From over here we think that over there
it is still nineteen forty five. But no –
for the people who live there it is just
their town which goes now by its Polish name.
A beautiful building in the centre
of the civic square has been turned into
a grocery shop.

Since the end of communism they get
a lot of Jewish tourists. One old man
showed us a Jewish cemetery. There
was nothing except a grassy slope with
a stream nearby. And some trees. Maybe they
were cherry trees? The old man would talk to
the guide and she would translate a quarter
of what he said. We put dollars in his hand
and wondered whose house
he lived in.

One cemetery was unusual.
Around the outside was a concrete wall,
broken in two by a jagged crack. In
the middle of the crack there was space. From
inside the wall you could see their wintery
Polish sky. We weren't sure whether this crack in the wall
was a sculpture or just neglect and if
it was a sculpture, what it meant. As a group
we are still divided.

Another day, we were walking in the
town square with our guide when she turned to us
and said, *We miss our Jews*. We didn't know
what to make of this
either.

I'm not sure what to call what I have done

When I describe what I have done, other poets look at me askance.
I chose the latest collection by a poet who has written hundreds
                                                    of poems but has
never hit the big time. I read all the poems in his latest collection
                                    and I wrote down all the
most beautiful words. If it was music it might be called 'sampling'.

As proxies for philosophers and people of all religions, I asked
                                four people to read all the
poems in the latest collection by the poet who has written
                            hundreds of poems but never hit
the big time and write down all the most beautiful words.
Any word or phrase which was chosen by three or more of us
                                            was saved.
As the person with the idea, I claimed the right to arrange these
                                    beautiful words into a
poem. I left spaces to stand in for all the ordinary bits.

For a short time I was content with my new poem and
                                undisturbed by the thought of the
most beautiful words, and the words chosen as beautiful by a
                                minority, mixing with all those
ordinary words in the original poems.
But last week, seeing that there was a full moon and many stars,
                                    *which I knew the moon
would soon obscure,* I took the latest collection by the poet who
                                had written hundreds of
poems but never hit the big time and I set fire to it on the beach.

Soon I will make a new poem from the few words which, by
                                chance, survived the flames

In the voice of Paul Celan reading *Todesfuge*, I hear a man led by his poem.

I hear his poems deeply, with my mouth. I hear him travelling East at night, alone. I hear him laying stone on stone. Each night he finds a dark shining heart and holds it in his hand. From this heart flows cunning. The voice of cunning wakes me from a dream. It comes from my own mouth.

I hear him laying stone on stone. Every exiled poet is a stone. Every place or person with more than one name is a stone. Every date is a stone. Every mother is a stone. Every blue eye is a stone. Every brown suit is a stone. Every photograph is a stone. Person-stone, book-stone, place-stone.

RIINA KATAJAVUORI (b. 1968) lives in Finland. She studied at the universities of Helsinki and Edinburgh and has an MA in literature. Since the appearance of her debut collection in 1992 she has published sixteen books (poetry, novels, short stories and children's books). Her poems have been translated into more than twenty languages.

The following poems are chosen from four collections: *Painoton tila* (The Weightless Space, 1998), *Koko tarina* (The Whole Story, 2001), *Kerttu ja Hannu* (Gretel and Hansel, 2007), and *Omakuvat* (Self-portraits, 2011).

SARKA HANTULA has translated many Finnish poets into English, including Olli Heikkonen, Jouni Inkala, Riina Katajavuori, Jyrki Kiiskinen, Tomi Kontio, Markku Paasonen, Helena Sinervo, Sirkka Selja, Anni Sumari, Saila Susiluoto, Mirkka Rekola, Ilpo Tiihonen, and Sirkka Turkka. She lives in Helsinki, Finland.

ANSELM HOLLO, born in Helsinki in 1934, was the author of some 40 books. He translated from Finnish, French, German and Swedish into English, and won several awards for his work as poet and translator. He was also one of the early translators of poetry by Allen Ginsberg, Gregory Corso and William Carlos Williams into German. He lived in the USA from 1967 until his death in 2013.

DAVID HACKSTON is a translator of Finnish and Swedish literature and drama. He graduated from University College London with a degree in Scandinavian Studies and now lives in Helsinki, where he works as a freelance translator. He is also a professional countertenor and specialises in the performance of early music.

Over the years I have often written about artists and self-portraits, and I have also been fascinated by stories such as 'Hansel and Gretel' by the Brothers Grimm, and by Maurice Sendak's *Where the Wild Things Are* – as well as the film version directed by Spike Jonze (see 'A boy reaches the monster island').

I also write about (strange) encounters and expectations, about my late grandmother, and all sorts of unrelated events and objects around me. Some poems, such as 'I eat a pepper that's not', had their birthplace in Budapest.

Poetry can also be a political medium. I wanted to write about the Beslan massacre in North Ossetia in 2004, but chose a very simple way to do it.

In 2005 I attended a translation workshop in Shetland, run by the Scottish Poetry Library and Literature Across Frontiers, where I made friends with Lise Sinclair, a poet and singer-songwriter from Fair Isle. It seemed that Fair Isle, or even the faint idea of it, had inspired me long before I visited the island, and it has remained a source of inspiration ever since I made my way there ('From the windowed veranda', 'I listened to the soundscape').

Every time I start a new book I feel I have to invent my poetic language anew. Poetry, for me, is not a narrative genre. It is all about the language: perspective, point of view, superimpositions, overlapping choices. So much material is always left on the cutting-room floor. For me, poetry is naming things or emotions or moments in a previously undiscovered way. 'Can we ever sufficiently assimilate/appreciate things if we have no vocabulary for them?'

Elin

A woman, reaching forward, offers
an apple impudently.
There's a corset lying on a chair
even though the bed has been made with care.

Today she speaks from the gut,
paints a different self-portrait:
lifts her chin up,
        gazes like a drill.
The halo of her hair aglow.

The eyes of the metropolis are glittering.
Inside her skirt she is
the master over herself.

Translated by Sarka Hantula

Translator's note: Elin Danielson-Gambogi (1861–1919) was a Finnish painter.

I eat a pepper that's not
yellow, red, green.
It's a lamp, it's a lantern, it has
a tapering shape,
it's bashful, its colour's timid,
like a candle, with a pallid glow
an afternoon in January.
I eat the pale yellow, lime lustre pepper,
it tastes of the sun, crisp, piquant.
I eat a plum, I eat a second plum,
I eat a third red plum,
I bite into the Hawaiian yellow flesh
and inside each of them a stone I'll treasure up.
I pick up a peach, as soft as the nape
of my child's neck, I slit it open
I cut it into dripping bits and drop them into kefir.

I eat my blazing, yellow and white meal
on a white tablecloth next to a red cupboard –
and I split a watermelon, I eat the red raspy
chunks, I let the black seeds trickle down,
the streets are glowing with thirty-four degrees,
and the juice of the melon is cool, I swallow it all.
Yellow trams are clattering down in the valley,
cherry trees are sagging, blackberries reaching out
above the pavements, my skin is hot,
moist, I won't wipe off the sweat, I find a tomato in the bowl,
I feel like laughing, such a funny tomato, I take a bite from its side,
a ball of light, bauble, it tastes of the sun too.
The sky is milk-white, peels on the table, a peach pit,
a green resounding shell, perfect for an instrument.
Thank you, I'm full, I'm replete, white curtains are fluttering,
thank you, I'm full, I'm replete.

Translated by Sarka Hantula

Superimpositions

Feeling: Joy, a phone call.
Doubt: One cannot govern anything but one's own department,
not even, for example, within one's own family.
Doubt 2, more generally: One cannot govern anything.
Home: bed, couch, table, sauna stove. The child's hair
is always matted.
She can't even keep her child's hair properly combed.
Message: We are strange.
Message 2: We are normal but our child has thin, woolly hair.
Milieu: the pine tree, the colour yellow, the bird.
No one taught us species. A reform ordered by the Education
Department. We'll run out of plants if all of them get picked and
pressed.
So they stay in nature, nameless.

Child, look, this is a flower. I am a human being, and you are a
child. This is a colour, and that is a material. That's precisely
what it feels like.

Light: A thousand stars, a lap, onto which one is lifted to look at
Saturn.
On the slope, a light pole, a bit like Dorian Gray's London.
Names: Ossian, Oscar, Dorian, Dora. Open Dora.
Names: Jenna, Jannika, Tilda, Tiona. Aleksi, Pieno, Tobias.

Translated by Anselm Hollo

Fathers and sons

There are fathers
who when the German shepherd gets whiny
take him out to the woods and shoot him.
There are fathers who toss kittens
one at a time against a concrete wall.
The sons stand by, alert as silver spoons,
watch closely, shout: BULL'S EYE!
and beat up the parquet floor
with their plastic hammers.

They measure things, the sons,
with their gauges and rulers.
Measure the tones of voice,
the number of words indicating attention,
the degree of tenderness shown
when Dad picks them up,
the ceiling of his patience
when they scramble upstairs.

Full of such metres they are,
the little sons.
'No put on clothes, want jammies,
now read good book
here in our new home.
Dad isn't home yet, he's still at work.'

Tomorrow, at the streetcar stop,
they'll tell the fathers to jump like rabbits.
And the whole world's fathers obey
and jump, jump hilariously,
with jutting incisors.

Translated by Anselm Hollo

Ninety-One

Where are you about to disappear, where are you now?
Behind what curtains are you pondering your half-sentences?
Where are your ferocity, your keen rhythm,
your intoxicating laugh disappearing?
You ask for dead people's telephone numbers, call them
again and again, and they die again for you, multiple times,
your sister who kicked you in the trundle bed,
your brother, his slender hands
when he taught you pat-a-cake.
You're living in a ghost movie, wandering
the strange white corridors of a ghost ship,
looking for familiar faces, finding strange people
engaged in incomprehensible tasks,
working their devices, speaking a foreign language, laughing
– you don't know at what. When you lie in your bed
someone appears on the headboard,
you look at the figure upside down, it looks like a giraffe,
or is it again that beautiful silent woman
who comes to look at you at nap time,
her gaze is frigid, no one else has seen her,
and neither would you like to see her, not yet.

Translated by Anselm Hollo

1.
morning tree,
                morning forest
your name, the most beautiful courtesy

don't say your name don't be lazy come close
don't smell of leather smell of leather and equine lather

2.
In one working day, the northern spruce trees had been cut down.
This made for more light, but we had moved here because of them,
we were younger then

A million waxwings just landed in the courtyard's maples
every single one seating itself to face the city

3.
do you remember when you walked home from school the maples
leaned towards you like rancid butter, the wild grapevine
the colour of rowanberry wine, the crooked fingers of the mountain
ash, you straightening them

swallow that orange now it knocks you out

Translated by Anselm Hollo

Beslan
for Dzerassa Gappojeva (9.1.1998–3.9.2004)

Bring water,
I am thirsty.
Bring tear water too,
sprinkle salt water both sides of the roadblock.
Bring a bright flower.
Bring Coca-Cola,
I am thirsty.

I am an ordinary pampered baby,
stuck out my tongue at you in the morning.

My hair looks untidy,
draw the ribbon tight.
Straighten my frilly collar,
it mustn't dangle today.

I'm a calf that was pulled out by its hooves,
you'll never forget that passage.
You almost fainted when I kicked you.
Phlegmy and bloody
I fell away from you.

Bring water,
bring a bright flower,
bring Coca-Cola.

I am your child,
I am the girl in the frilly blouse and flowers in my hair.
I am a child forever.
But do you know, mother,
so are all the children of all other mothers.
Even when grown up, forever children to their mothers.

Touch the red granite with your hand.
Is it cold?
The sun has been blazing all day.
So the granite must be warm now.
Warm and smooth it is.

You bring water, you bring a flower, you bring Coca-Cola.

The night will be clear.
I am blue smock flower hair girl,
I am holding balloons in my hands.

There were stars on the ceiling of the gym.

Translated by Anselm Hollo

Crow Grabs Poet's Scalp

He was jogging past the Peace Memorial. A poet, he was running in Kaivopuisto Park. A youngster, he was on his accustomed Sunday hike in Helsinki's southern developments. The proximity of the sea was an incentive. It was a fine, steely grey day. From its heavy cloudy stagnation the evening had turned towards night. The passenger vessel terminal called up persistent memories of youthful travels: they were a blend of festivity and Dickens. The drinks had names like Black Russian, Bloody Mary, and there was one consisting of Coca-Cola and banana liqueur. Its cloying taste of promises could still be felt on the tongue.

From the Observatory Hill, a murder of crows rushed down and directed its route without hesitation across the poet's trail. He kept up a steady pace, contemplating a tennis match. The dirty grey and black birds made a lot of noise above his head. In those days it was up to the poet to take care of himself. Co-ordination & balance equals mental balance. A strong gust of air passed by both ears, wings beat on his cheeks, he felt claws in his hair. His ponytail was not long enough to whip the crow's tail. This was happening right now, and to him. Did a tired crow want a ride? And how did it want to settle on his head?

Together, they rose up into the air. Amazement kept him from feeling cold. He pulled a digital camera out of his belt pack and shot aerial views of the ever more distant lights of Helsinki. The sea looked like a cosy counterpane. He trusted the crow. He would wash his hair when this was over. Pandemics and so on. The crow dropped him into a black rubber boat full of activists. They had been trained to deal with such things. Together, they boarded a corporation vessel and prevented the cutting down of primeval forests. Finally, he landed in Estonia. Now the poet sits in the library of Rakvere or among the ruins of Viljandi. The young man has become well-rounded. Life gains different liminal conditions when the perspective suddenly changes.

Translated by Anselm Hollo

In the forest, Hansel tells Gretel about owls

Even if you tie a bandage around its eyes
an owl can catch a mouse or a mole.
An owl flies without sound,
its wings do not swoosh.
The most beautiful owls
are the eagle owl and the long-eared one,
but no owl could be called ugly.

That rabbity sound is made by the pearly owl.
It is calling for a mate,
it is not a rabbit, it is an owl.

The female Ural owl does not hesitate
to grab a person's head
with its sharp talons fully deployed.
This feels like being hit with a piece of firewood.

The hawk owl has the worst temper.
If a human approaches its nest
the mother strikes the back of their head
like a cannonball.
Then you must throw yourself down
at the foot of a juniper bush
or else risk losing your eyes.

Such is the family life of the owls.

Translated by Anselm Hollo

Self-portrait 18.3.2009, 1.20 p.m.

Shiny hair loose, streaming across shoulders, a strand forming a
letter C at the back. Peaceful, inquisitive, green eyes, if anything
closer together than set apart. Lips exhausted, a faint gloss
spread over them. Fingers hold the notebook in her lap like a
shell, index finger and middle finger in a twisted grip around a
biro, as if in fear of drowning. Slender wrists, large palms. She
looks sleepy. Wrapped up warm, red, red-brick, green-dotted
tunic, blouse, cardigan. Eyes and cheeks seem like odd pairs.

Translated by David Hackston

From the windowed veranda you can see a white lighthouse
behind a soft, white horse. As I remember it, peppermint tea is
steaming in my hands. The trees do not obstruct the view; they
are not there at all, there is only a flat, pale greenness, like at the
football juniors' air-inflated hall, in the never-ending cold. A
cool, bleak, silent dome of mist stealthily descends from above
and beneath the daylight, and the eight-seater plane goes to sleep.
The lighthouse beacon is flickering, spinning. No one sounds the
foghorn any longer; now there are only radars, sheltered journeys,
safeguarded in so many ways. The horse raises its head; a
woman purls a pattern into a jumper. It is a complicated,
colourful task; I could do it too if I'd been born here. I wouldn't
weed out the vegetables' tender roots, and my soul would be
more unflinching, though it is rather, even now.

Translated by David Hackston

A boy reaches the monster island where bellowing and conflict
rage among the people. The monsters long for a leader, for
authority, a higher power. And the monster island isn't an easy
place to rule. After all, who would want to be king? One might
even love the monster that smashed those honeycomb habitations
that we all struggled to put together. The boy makes a good
ruler, because he plays with the monsters and spurs them into
battles in which both he and the monsters can use the full extent

of their strength. The boy is a wise ruler, for he accepts that he is not a real king but an everyday one.

Translated by David Hackston

I listened to the soundscape, far from the frequency of my own fire station. I've misplaced my sound notes, but to close my eyes was much indeed, to lie down on a stony wharf or some other such thing leading out into the sea. A lamb had lost its mother, or the mother was bleating noisy instructions, and I listened to this dialogue for a long time. Along the northern shore of the island, the sea roared differently from how I had imagined. The birds all had three names: in the official language, in the local dialect and in Finnish, so everything was unclear, the arctic skua, the puffins, the black-backed gulls, the common eider – and I could appreciate them, though everything was so non-conceptual, as there were no real words/names for anything and I didn't recognise the species. Can we ever sufficiently assimilate/ appreciate things if we have no vocabulary for them or if we have neither guidebook nor ornithology book to hand?

Translated by David Hackston

The bewilderment that to other people I am someone, though to myself I am undefined. The slanted, pink morning light on the snowy window ledge has turned golden.

The protagonist exists in a constant state of near collapse, one that consumes the mind when travelling alone, when the watertight certainty of eventually returning home must be constructed. In the early hours snow-ploughs scrape menacingly across the asphalt.

At the summer cottage the others retire, and the protagonist retires too. Fragility descends, pyjama-pretending. We pretend we can survive anything at all, the cottage, spending the night there, dangling on a lifeline of helpful phone numbers, the emergency services, there amid the forest's own life and sound.

There must surely be astronauts, cosmonauts, surgeons who all lack such inbuilt traits (fear of the dark, fear of space, fear of the emptiness, the bottom of the sea, fear of the night and the starry sky, spatial anxiety).

The protagonist is documented on film or captured in a novella. Right now, there on the cutting-room floor is the section in which the protagonist is spinning wordlessly in a ball chair. In the background, a tape speaks the protagonist's thoughts out loud.

Translated by David Hackston

DAVID KRUMP is a graduate of the MSt in Creative Writing at the University of Oxford and has received the Ruth Lilly Fellowship from *Poetry*, the Poetry Foundation/Newberry Library Fellowship in American Poetry, and the Lorine Niedecker Award. His poetry has appeared in *Poetry*, *Poetry Review* and *Verse*. His plays have been produced in small- and medium-sized theatres and filmed by Wisconsin Public Television. He edits *Poets & Artists*, works in politics and the not-for-profit sector, and co-curated a monthly literary series (with William Stobb) for seven years. He lives in La Crosse, Wisconsin.

I like poems that do not take themselves too seriously or expect to survive for hundreds of years. I like people that take themselves very seriously and expect to survive through the day. Beyond my concerns with time and seriousness, I can say that, having re-read them, these poems feel burdened to me. Timidly, I almost want to apologise for their weight, but sooner or later one must own what one has written. Heavy things happen in my proximity and reality occasionally girds my writing. When this happens, intentionally or otherwise, I feel enabled – perhaps cartoonishly protected – by writing, because when written, experiences appear manageable and possess margins, borders, beginnings and ends. 'This is where the experience starts and this is where it ends,' a poem says. 'Thanks, poem,' I say. 'You've made this experience, whether real or not, easier for me.' I do not intend to suggest that everything should be or could be ease-centric in my writing, but poems could do far worse than ease along their writer's life. I suppose a poem could wound the elderly or corrupt the young. Without informing me, my work might wish to wound and corrupt, but it can't. Not yet. Still, I think it is a good thing that I distrust my work now and again. I showed a few different drafts of this note to my friend Bill. Bill is a great poet, as far as contemporary American poets go. Regarding my other versions of this note, none of which have been incorporated here, Bill wrote in an email, 'Of your statements, I like the first one better. They both sound a little *cynical* about poetry, which may be the tension you're feeling in them. Lord knows, it's understandable to be cynical about poetry, but maybe it would seem a little too contradictory in an actual poetry anthology. And anyway, do you really feel that way about them? Disposable?' Good point. My work isn't disposable – not exactly – and I am very grateful for it, even while it causes me conflict. Bill reminds me of things I should feel more or less of. In this way, Bill is like a poem.

Notes from a Journey

We died during a train wreck
outside your winter village
the word *Mary* on our tongues.

Apples. It was apples our mothers
placed in our pale hands.
Apples and smoked ham sticks.

Oranges did not exist then.

We had heard of *Oranges* in our classes
as we had heard of *Elegy* and *Cincinnati*.
Our mothers calmly, terrified, kissed us.

On the platform we were strange
creatures, guarding giant cases
containing our lessons and pants.

We boarded as our belongings
were loaded by thick-wristed men.
Pull and puff went the carriage.

The rest goes crack, goes under.
A young nun points to beads.
The sharp dark, cold water
and far inside, this thought of beds.

An Ample Tree

In preparation for his simple death
my brother gathers his uniforms, dried boots,
a collectible Bible and apples fallen
from an ample tree. These he places
into a discarded oak barrel he's pulled
from the slough. The oak staves have swollen
tight. He drops the apples in last and asks
that I keep the barrel, a gift. *No, right
beside the table-vice*, he advises

when I make to roll it to the corner,
empty but for the push-broom's bristles.

In garage light, he twitches, hands over
his revolver, two dense pounds heavier
than it looks, little thing. How mistaken my offer
to store this barrel must seem to him. I'm often
mistaken – not an *ample* tree, but a *maple* tree
drops these oddest apples, accolades of the fall.

Failed Sidekick's Dilemma

You promised we'd find ourselves
an illustrator but you're content
to peel an orange as buildings topple
and search parties arrange
to scrabble through rubble.

You are uninterested. I can tell
anyone we meet our real names. You won't
fuss if I remove the cape, the mask.
Will you weep, should I return alone
to the catastrophe of mere citizenry?

I! Your sidekick whose utility
belt holds your necessaries –
moist towelettes, mini toothbrush,
tweezers, Tums, Tic-Tacs.

You laugh at it now: *That?*
That fanny pack? But you promised
to teach me the grappling hook
and how the jet car works.

You guaranteed me one groggy night
I'd regain consciousness to notice
my limbs bound at their ends
and my body tossed into a wire basket
descending into a smelting basin
in a steel refinery or other enemy dark place.

You promised I could repeat
our code words: *It is 1979. It is 1979
and I have not been born yet.*

You were supposed to save me then.

Prometheus at the Checkpoint

They search his goatskin bag.
He empties his pockets, turns them out.
He removes his shoes and belt buckle too.
He's hidden the fire in his mouth.

Love Song for Rural Idiots

All winter Brother B constructs two clocks
in the monastery shop. Planed pine
in hand wallops the heart. Tonight
Brother Bernard drinks many beers
while driving empty county roads, pointing
out worthy fishing holes. Not long we do this
before a state trooper tases and tackles him.

Pulled over, Brother B decides to run. To run oddly
like a sinner's ghost from the voice of God.
His brown robes caught on ditch branches
that held him. I watch from the monastery
truck, through the swept open driver's door
from which he leapt – a uniformed knee,
hard-down between his shoulders. The trooper yelled.
I blinked in the passenger seat.
Brother B's prayers, the March air.
After questions, the trooper lets me go.

I walked the sideways miles to this bar, waiting
two hours before calling the abbot about our habit.

Ophelia Soft

There are new ghosts
in the Mississippi
and all day they play
unimaginable, underwatery
games with each other.
Come night, the moon
releases them, old and new,
from the grip of the river.
Then old drowned Sioux
and new suicides
chase weightless spirits
of black and brown bison
through our bedrooms.
Perhaps those who died
in what we understand
as accident do not realise
their conclusions. Every
night they waver through
small-town side-streets
back to the small taverns.
They stand impossibly still
with a twenty-dollar bill
dripping on the bar, wondering
why no one will serve them.
Among the living, few hear
this tired pounding on the bar
or those desperate whispers of theirs:
What did I do the last time I was here
which has me so now ignored?
Alley cats' ears pitch up, vibrate
into double votives when the ghosts
float sobbing on by, lonely as water
in the beginning. In the beginning
there was a vast and formal formlessness,
then waters, rivers, ground
the formlessness down,
separated the dead
from the living.

Poem Written in Realtime

We learn in January to believe
in the deserted body
on rural church steps.

We know now new snow falls
at five in the morning. Empty acres
across the road whistle snow.

Her body now is more than a body
just as a fist is a hand gone mad.
Here are white flowers and red.

The snow-plow driver arrives early
in darkness to clear the church
parking lot for Sunday services.

From his parked car, traveling chaplain
can't believe the county trooper
unspools yellow tape, barring the entrance
steps. Detectives sweep away snow.

Snow on the empty body, empty
church. The mustached detectives
discover so much: this winter will last
                            our lives.

One Crow

For ten minutes, midfield, a man adjusts the coulters on his
plow. In a yellowed pasture, a small figure leads a broken beast
by the bridle, walking it in figure eights.

The police chief of the small town sits at his dining room table –
radio, low squelch, ceramic cup, hot and squat. Warm autumn
weather stirs several brown bats in cedar eaves. Black soil curls
up behind the plow and breaks on itself like boat-wake. Quail
and sparrow rise from flat chaff in the tractor's path and settle
down to feast on stray kernels several rows west.

While someone bends to a gun and one thin crow outside the
farmhouse window turns to the bright snap, grows suddenly fat,
and lifts off, I am thinking about the Powers, those beings who
tuck grass to sleep, who stir horned owls alert at night, who
guide slow worms through earth with tiny lanterns.

A Stream

B frees his fiddle from its leather case
and walks across the dark charms of the farmyard.
A hears him playing to the Jersey calves
and highway weeds. How strange this afternoon,
scraping the silo floor clean for tomorrow
A daydreamed a reductive sleep, because lately
in his end-of-the-world dreams, he smells diesel
studies windrows winding over northern fields
hears the world re-tuning its cat-gut heart.
Then comes blood from birds, chaff of rye
fermata, then mostly moonlight on several spirits
swimming in the anxious double stream.

Old Geometry

When we have been dead
one year, meet us in the garden
of fallen farm implements. Near the shadow
the barn's cupola casts through the calving pasture
at noon in July as slant swallow shadows enter
the maple's larger shadow.

Bring us water in the metal pail with the good handle.
Place copper cups on ten fence posts. Pour the middle
news of bright things born.

We will trade for this news five givens.

FRANCES LEVISTON's first book of poems, *Public Dream*, was published by Picador in 2007 and shortlisted for the T.S. Eliot Prize. Her poems have appeared in the *Times Literary Supplement*, the *London Review of Books* and various anthologies. She reviews for the *Guardian* and the *TLS*. www.francesleviston.co.uk

'Bishop in Louisiana' was first published in the *Guardian*. 'Sulis' was first published in *Poetry London*. 'Woodland Burial' was commissioned and published by the National Gallery.

These six poems come from the manuscript of my second book, *Disinformation*. 'Disinformation' refers to '[the] dissemination of deliberately false information, esp. when supplied by a government or its agent to a foreign power or to the media' and to 'false information so supplied' (*OED*). I am interested in the questionable truthfulness of poetry, how it might exist in spite of or in protest against a globalised economy of knowledge, and whether it may itself be a kind of disinformation.

'GPS' and 'IUD' were both written to counterpoint the utilitarianism of their titles. 'Kassandra' was inspired by a visit to the Chalkidiki peninsula in northern Greece. 'Bishop in Louisiana' is part of a tradition of 'X in Z' poems, where X is a dead poet and Z is an unlikely location: in this case, the south-eastern coast of the US in the aftermath of the Deepwater Horizon disaster.

While attempting to translate the Old English poem 'The Ruin', I read about its connection to the Roman ruins at Bath, and about the *interpretatio Romana* whereby the indigenous Celtic goddess Sulis was fused with the Roman goddess Minerva. These circumstances, and the idea of syncretic identification, lie behind 'Sulis'.

'Woodland Burial' was commissioned by the National Gallery, which asked me to respond to Titian's Diana paintings and Ovid's *Metamorphoses*. I focused on *The Death of Actaeon*. Rather than pursue the traditional motif of the deer and hounds, I imagined that Diana destroyed Actaeon simply by refusing to acknowledge him as distinct from the woodland backdrop, enabling me to explore the power of suppression, denial and silence in the construction of political narratives.

GPS

Like a wet dream this snow-globe was a gift
to myself. It rides shotgun in the passenger seat

or stuck to the dashboard, swirling and swirling
across the carpet of potholes to my house.

Its mantelpiece matryoshka
wears an inscrutable face:

there's no telling how many dolls deep she goes
beyond her one red peanut-shell,

her pupa's lacquered shine,
superglued to a painted knoll, brilliantly magnified

by an atmosphere of cerebrospinal fluid
under the smooth glass dome's museum,

a solid case of ozone.
When I do a U-turn it triggers another storm.

Her compass boggles. Lie down there in that drift,
little girl, you're feeling strangely warm,

and something big is about to make sense
if we just keep going in the opposite direction.

IUD

This gadget intrudes so nothing else can. It froths
the way a widget froths beer, agitant,

dispenses with the problem of abstinence – *don't* –
and plants a dull pea under the mattress.

Childless. Sleepless. Rings on cushions do this too,
diamonds in the toilet. *I placed a jar in Tennessee;*

in the wilderness I buried my witch's bottle,
half-full of screws, pins, piss and curse blood,

keeping a promise in a place I've forgotten.
A prize in every box! A mine in a mitten. Automated

night-time sprinkler system. The walk-in wardrobe's
coat-hangers cannon and tinkle, turning to hooks.

Kassandra

We touch down in Siviri, on Kassandra,
the first spiral arm. A mantis dries in the myrtle.
Moths drag their abdomens through the fluid sand
in eternity symbols. The sea, antagonised
a cloudy blue, banks long drifts
of ticker-tape seaweed up against the pilings.
The air smells of salt, and the sweetness of pines
that weep thin syrup to the compound earth,
their long, pliable, pale green needles
managing to droop and spike at the same time.

White skies overcast, and calm, and close.
The beach loses contrast like a film too long exposed:
nacre-coloured, ivory, silver, shell.
The lukewarm water doesn't wave, it breathes.
I lie flat on a flat cool dune,
my cardigan for a pillow, ear-down. The raised
spine of my book makes a rampart
where a tiny brown spider sits, proprietorially
taking the view. Sometimes he puts
his four front legs in the air and feels around,
checking the humidity, or hailing a friend.
When the sun touches him he shines like resin,
half-transparent. His face is a shield,
almost the size of the hooded crows' hoods
of beaten mail, where they mooch beyond him,
then jump into the air like they're jumping on to the ground.

Further down the beach, teenage boys
are dismantling a tiki-bar's wooden umbrellas.
They dig long palings out of the sand,
kept damp all season where they sharpen
to pencil-points at the ends, and rest them on their sides.
The shades, made of matted old tinder,
tile in overlapping panels towards us –
a solar field or a shield-wall at distance, the scales
of a lizard seen up close. Then the boys
carry them into the gloomy bar-room, in columns,
lightly as leafcutter ants delivering
doilies of privet to their underground posts.

Eagerly the restaurateur by the taxi rank
welcomes us, his only patrons, to a blue-painted table
and disposable white paper table-cloth.
Stray cats leap and drop into the garbage dumpers.
Across the gulf we can see Mount Olympus
melt the red sun like a bath-pearl on its peak.
The Russian girl who serves us is blonde and sad,
her eyes, born too far apart,
watery and pale as peeled cucumber. She wants to talk.
The chickpea soup and the octopus are good.
Her best friend married an Englishman
and moved away last year. There was a terrible fire here
that burnt the whole village down to the stone.
Everybody saw it happen on the news.
Things haven't been the same. She sounds like someone
from another time, someone with an open wound.

Ouzo turns white when it touches ice,
like people's eyes in the presence of angels.
The cubes revolve in its milky emulsion.
Tomorrow the sea will be plaster and the sky plaster-cast.
Already three cafés and the pâtisserie are closed.
An old man sits at the end of the quay,
watching the caïques darken through his cataracts.
He catches fish too small to eat.
The rollers turn white when they hit the rocks.

Bishop in Louisiana

Twelve days since I took up my post in this village,
a handful of clapboard houses crowded round the harbour
and the concrete yards glittering with scales
where church groups serve up grits and tamales
from long trestle tables and the interiors of white vans.

I myself eat at the hotel, beef, pasta, anything but fish,
watching the black sea break foamlessly
against the chemical barricade. On its surface orange curds
ride like surfboards or children's life-preservers.
After dinner I take my coffee in the privacy of my suite.

There is little to accomplish here. I walk on the beach
where the nests of common terns driven upwind to breed
are marked with red flags mounted on popsicle sticks,
hundreds of them, bunting in the wind. Each nest is no more
than a dint in the sand, easily made with a fist.

Yesterday I saw a dead sea-turtle turning to soup
inside its own shell. I am not immune to the irony of this.
I write cheques for the fishermen fitting their boats
with booms to skim the water, and speak to sad newscasters
under a flypast of helicopters and a crop-duster salute.

Try to imagine what a hundred million litres means.
You can't. At night, before bed, in the surprisingly deep bath,
I push my big toe into the streaming faucet
and feel its pressure build to a hot, relentless gush,
nightmarishly pleasurable, like pissing myself in my sleep.

Sulis

1

When Sulis rose from the open ground
and entered Minerva, she mastered that shape
with such perfection she seemed to vanish
under history's golden heel,

as if Minerva sank one foot in the fountain
and poured her rival off –
only to hear in her victory-moment
a worshipper offer verbatim the prayer

Sulis drew from his mouth before,
as lovers change loved ones more than words;
only to find her eyes in the mirror
swam with someone else's tears.

2

The gap between Senuna's teeth,
which took a thick coin or the edge of a sword,
the slit between worlds, a problem
and a wish, gushed with water day and night

into the trampled midden she ruled:
Sulis's mother, her predecessor,
recipient of plaques and the clasps of hoods,
songs and bones, the model of a lion,

who vanished after Sulis did.
There are several ways of dissolving:
to soak yourself in the baths is one;
to let the mud meet above your head is another.

3

That owl gone hunting is the ghost
of Desdemona, or at least her after-image:
corneas domed, a dropped
hanky breast in the dark. Sulis would love her

credulous glare, the warm
mouse making its way down her gullet,
surrendering fur and ears and claws
the better to join her entourage,

and the story of how she started flying
her own feather bolster and long white ribbon,
displaced from the palace
not by a mistress, but by an avatar.

4

Pellets indistinguishable from seed-husks
tighten round an emptiness.
Hands without another hand to hold make fists.
Under the willows

discarded vessels, void of fluid,
ache for Sulis to love them again, not leave them
there in the succulent grass.
Already she is forgetting their faces;

she leans to spit in her lover's mouth
and makes a bridge, a casual suspension
involving them both,
like spider-silk draped from cactus to cactus.

5

Here they are, Pallas, Minerva,
with hair so heavy it bows their heads
and grey thick ankles they cool where the river
slows its rush in a kind of pond.

Nothing beyond their bodies concerns them,
nothing beyond the pools of light
their own lamps throw.
They did what they could in their time, and now

the boys who briefly rest in their shadows
cannot matter much to them,
as much as the veiled
flies on cows' faces bother the cows.

6

Water's not particular, but where it passes is;
water like wisdom resists capture,
never complacent, revising itself
according to each new container it closes.

The heart thrives on syncresis. Sulis
hearts each man she kisses,
each costume she wears, each nakedness;
like formal dresses

she carries them with her into the cloud,
its floating parade
of people who laundered her difficult feelings
until she put them aside.

Woodland Burial

Thrown water touched him and where it touched it said
his body was the same brownness leaves turn
when autumn is upon us, a swept-up heap
trembling where it stood,
that when the huntress concentrated
trees, tree-shadows, underbrush and bushes made a wood
and it was ever thus, that nothing can be other than as known
by a god, no truth a lie, no death long sleep.

Poised with springy longbow drawn
and back to the sun, the one who had revealed her form
from landscape or eyes
independent as a streak of white paint on a mirror
held him on her gaze
and held the torn canopy of clouds on the water
as she might have kept a spoonful of honey in the warm
fold of her tongue before it dissipated.

Not the greatest possible harm,
which needs to be known and named as such
to achieve its end, not what he fled, but the unofficial crime,
the moment she let her attention crop
those deep recursive avenues of beech to a backdrop
he broke against, confused,
so nothing in the landscape escaped his touch
and nothing left of him was in the picture she composed.

PETER MACKAY is a writer, academic and broadcaster. He has a PhD from Trinity College, Dublin, and has written widely on contemporary Scottish and Irish literature, as well as Scottish Gaelic literature. Originally from the Isle of Lewis, he now lives in Edinburgh.

Beyond my mother's house on the Isle of Lewis – the house I grew up in – the tarmac gives way to a peat road, holed and stony, which bends out of sight over a hill past the standing stones of Stein-a-Cleit, the remains of an Iron Age settlement or tomb: no one has definitively identified what it was. Past the stones are open moor and lochs for ten miles, an expanse uninhabited till the stretched-out settlements on the east of the island: miles of heather, bog, bog-cotton, the hint of deer, the insistent summer hum and haze of cleg and midgie. Apart from the transatlantic jets passing overhead – the stark skies are rarely without at least one fading tendril of jet-smoke – there are few signs of modernity.

But this is an utterly created landscape. Over millennia, the great forest of Lewis was burned, the peat stripped down metres; the land is now veined through by peat banks, with the traces of *àirighean* (the sheilings used in the transhumance of previous generations) and flattened, corroded hulks of metal, all that remain of the Hillman Imps, caravans and grocers' vans dragged or driven last century to be left to rot there, while serving as a shelter during each summer's peat-cutting. Occasionally, the blade of a *tairisgeir* will still cut through the skeleton of a bird, preserved in the peat, a boned cave or shell of air; very occasionally now, as the moor passes out of common or frequent use.

Lewis is a place of many languages – the names and nouns are relics and scorings of different cultures: Norse, Gaelic, Scottish, Anglo-Saxon. And it is a place of many departures: its seas and horizons are wide and wild, luxuriously seductive and then terrifying in their changeability.

It is now sixteen years since I lived on Lewis; I have been a confirmed urbanite in Glasgow, Barcelona, Dublin, Belfast and now Edinburgh, and doubt how much I am still part of the idealised trans-historical place of summer I have just described, and how much it is part of me.

The Log Roller

You are the century's logger and reiver
balanced between English and Gaelic,
a frontiersman with each foot on a log
rolling inexorably down the Mackenzie.
Sometimes your speech is schizoid
but sometimes it is subtle, right
and winding, as when John Munro wrote
about mob-caps of snow on the mountains
of Assynt in the mid-1910s,
in Gaelic, the English unsaid.
But like a horse slick-stepped yet slipshod
in two styles you stumble and falter
unless – no turning back – you go further,
add cant to parole to langue,
and skipping from word to word, log to log
roll your unbearable haul up the river.

Logorrhoea

Bu tu gaol òir m' òige
do ghàire ghaoil mar fhir-chlis
an geamhradh gorm Leòdhais
mo ghaol, mo rìbhinn òg.

Nan robh mi nam fhear-dhìon
's chan e fear-bholg, fear-chuideachd,
bhithinn air tairgsinn dhut gaol maireannach
an àite logorrhoea.

Agus a-nis tha mo ghaol aig tèile
mar bu chòir 's mar bu dual,
ged a tha do sholais nam speuran
a' lainnireadh thar a' chaoil.

Logorrhoea

You were the gold love of my youth
your laugh love like the northern lights
in the blue Lewis winter
my love, my young love.

If I was, say, a musketeer,
and not a wastrel and a fool,
I'd have given you love that lasted
instead of logorrhoea.

And now my love is another's
as is right, as should be;
but your lights are still in my skies
glittering across the kyle.

Na Dorsan

Tha na dorsan a' dùnadh sna bùithtean anmoch,
luchd-dìon mar shagartan aig na glasan.
'S e obair phearsanta a th' ann baile a chruthachadh
nad ìomhaigh fhèin. Obair làithean fada
a' coiseachd shràidean, a' faicinn dhuilleagan a' fàs
agus a' bàsachadh nan leum-sneachd' dathte,
a' cunntadh nan argamaidean, a' dearbhadh peant ùr
air soidhneachan, a' smìoradh smùr glas air ballachan
ruadha, a' leigeil às cait fhiadhaich d' amharais,
's tìgearan d' eud, a' teicheadh bho phantaran
ann an leabharlann do chuimhne, a' tomhas
casan fada caileagan na bliadhna sa 's an-uiridh,
a' sìneadh do bhreugan mar ùir air àrd-eaglais,
a' lorg nam faclan a chruthaicheas an call.

The Doors

The doors are closing in the late town,
security guards like priests at the locks.
It is private work creating a town
in your own image, the work of long days
of walking streets, watching leaves grow
and die in a fall of colour,
counting arguments, confirming new paint
on signs, smearing grey soot on red walls,
releasing the wild cats of your suspicion,
the tigers of jealousy, running from panthers
in the library of your memory, measuring
the long legs of this year's girls and last year's,
spreading your lies like soil on the cathedral,
looking for words to construct a loss.

Bàta Taigh Bàta

Rinn Màiri Mhoireasdan seòmar-cèilidh
à sparran tràlair a h-athair:
sin neo am fàgail nam malcadh
an àiteigin air cladach cèin.

Nan cuireadh tu do bhas air an darach
bha e eadar sàl agus gainneamh;
nan gnogadh tu air,
dhèanadh e *scut*.

Chrom sailthean an tobhta-bhràghad
ris a' mhuir, dà mhile air falbh;
gach oidhche ghluais an taigh
ann am bòchain, a' tarraing air acair,

dh'fhuaimneadh mic-talla tron fhiodh
mar ghlaoidhean uilebheistean-mara.
Dh'fhàs polaip agus grom fo sgeilp an TBh,
rinn an uinneag dùrdan drabasta,

fhuair a'ghaoth an similear mun amhaich
a' feuchainn ri tharraing o mharachadh,
fon bhòrd-chofaidh bha stòbhan-air-bòrd
a' cagar gu gnù, ann an ceannairc.

Chumadh cas-cheum
sean mharaiche a' chamhanaich,
thairngeadh ròpanan an latha.

Ri tìde, fuasglaidh i na snaidhmean,
gus a giùlan fhèin tron t-sìl,
thèid a briseadh air an t-slighe.

Boat House Boat

Mary Morrison made her living room
from the spars of her father's trawler;
it was either that or leave it to rot
on some distant shore.

If you smoothed your palm on the oak
it was between sand and salt:
if you chapped it,
it gave out a *scut*.

The beams of the bow curved out
towards the sea, two miles away.
Each night the walls would catch
in the tide and pull on anchor,

echoes would sound through the wood,
like the calls of sea-monsters.
Polyps and coral started to form under the TV shelf,
the bay-window murmured bawdily,

the wind caught the chimney by the scruff
and tried to lift it from its moorings,
under the coffee table stowaways gathered
whispering in sullen mutiny.

A sailor's boottaps
keeps the smallhours;
the pulling of ropes fills the day.

Over time, she will work open the knots,
force herself towards the sea,
be broken on the way.

Ball-sampaill

Canar gum bristeadh gearra-bhall
deigh nam marannan a tuath –
a sleagh mar phìc a' sgrìobadh
san uisge reòite ioma-uaine –
an tòir air mhurcan agus shìolagan,
a sgiathan crùbte ga sparradh
tro chriostailean solais a' phòla
a dh'fhàsadh air a bhian,
agus gun do dhùin an deigh
os cionn a' cholca, a thum 's a shlìob
mar dadam ann an *clinamen*
air neo aingeal na thuiteam,
's an uachdar a' fàs nas tighe 's nas tighe.
Fhathast uaireannan fon dheighe
cluinnear cacradh nam mìle gob.

Aon là thèid mi a' sealg le slat, dubhan
agus dineamait. Bu toil leam
mo chrògan fhaighinn air an iasg-eun,
a chnàimhean sgaoileadh fad 's farsaing –
dhan Mhet, dhan Kelbhingrove –
ugh a reic o a brù airson leth fhortain,
a bian a lìonadh le gainmheach
gus acrachadh ann an seo, an-dràsta,
gus glugair a sgòrnain a chlàradh.

Specimen

They say the gairfowl would break
through the ice of the northern seas –
its spear like a pick hacking
at the frozen celeste and turquoise –
in search of lumpsuckers and sandlances,
its stunted wings propelling itself
through the crystals of polelight
that would grow on its pelt,
and that the ice closed over the auk,
which dived and swerved
like an atom in its *clinamen*
or an angel mid-fall
as the crust grew thicker and thicker.
Under the ice you can still hear
the crackle of a thousand beaks.

One day I will go hunting with rod,
hook and dynamite. I would like
to get my hands on the fishbird
and share its bones far and wide –
with the Met, the Kelvingrove –
sell the egg from its womb
for a small fortune,
and fill its skin with sand:
to anchor it in the here and now,
to arrest the gurgle in its throat.

An Tobar

Bidh thu a' tilleadh gach là
dhan tobar air oir a' bhaile,
ach dha-rìribh chan eil e ann –
's tha agad ri a chruthachadh
on phronnas fiodha 's beatha,
's spaidreach chlachan.

Dimàirt cleachdaidh tu masg
de Lego agus breugan,
sìlidh 's corduroy;
là-eigin eile, stàilinn Tholedo,
pàintidh, faclan àiteachail,
itealan gearra-bhaill.

Chan e dealbh-sgàthain
a chì thu caog-shùileach
san fhuaran ach sgeulachd
toinnte na bhloigh
a tha gad innse claon
gach trup a tha thu ga h-aithris.

Gun fhios dhut cha thog thu
an aon tobar dà thuras;
a-chaoidh chan fhaigh thu a-rithist
blas an aon bhùirn.

The Well

You return each day to the well
on the edge of the village,
but it's not really there
and you have to rebuild it
from the detritus of wood and life
and stones scattered around.

Tuesday you use a mix
of Lego and lies,
jam and corduroy;
another day, Toledo steel,
pottery skelfs, agricultural terms
and auk feathers.

It is not a reflection you see
blinking in the deeps
but a twisted story
that tells you squint,
each and every time
you repeat it.

Without knowing it
you won't build the same well twice,
won't ever taste again
from the pull.

ÁDÁM NÁDASDY was born in 1947 in Budapest, Hungary, and has lived there all his life. He has a degree in English and Italian, and is Professor of Linguistics. He writes poetry in his native Hungarian. He also translates plays from English into Hungarian, in particular Shakespeare (nine plays so far), but also Wilde, Shaw, and Osborne.

CHRISTOPHER WHYTE, born in 1952, has translated Pasolini, Rilke and Tsvetaeva into English. His fifth poetry collection, in Scottish Gaelic, will appear later this year. He is also the author of four novels in English. Since 2005 he has lived in Budapest, Hungary, where he writes and translates full-time.

I think my poetic style can be called conservative, as I like to use traditional rhymed forms such as the sonnet (still practicable in Hungarian because the language easily lends itself to metre and rhyme, even classic hexameters). So I am no innovator or revolutionary. I use normal punctuation and correct spelling. On the other hand I aim at making my diction, my choice of words (often taken from the modern colloquial language), as well as my subject matter, as provocatively 'unpoetic' as possible. I write about door-knobs, tram drivers, or God serving me dinner. Mainly people: I love people, I find them enormously exciting. In this respect I learnt a lot from Shakespeare, who thought likewise. I also like to write funny things – better laugh than cry.

I began writing poems at the age of 29, and did not publish anything till I was 34 – quite late for a lyrical poet. The reason was that my main interest, both in life and in poetry, is love; but, being gay, I needed time to find ways to express this within the 'main-stream' poetic tradition of Hungarian. Also, you had to be tactful and discreet in the 1970s, and doubly so in Eastern Europe. But times have changed. I have published six volumes of poetry so far, and I also appear more or less regularly in the major Hungarian literary magazines. Recently I had a few poems in *PN Review*.

I was married when young, and have two daughters (and several grandchildren!). I am a believing Catholic, or perhaps I should say I believe in God and go to a Catholic church. Some of my poems tackle the personal relationship a person may establish with God, somewhat illegally, so to speak, behind the Church's back. For almost twenty years my partner was a Jewish man, whose self-chosen death is a theme of several of my poems. My present civil partner is a doctor, who is currently working in London, so I often stay in England – a country I have always loved. I have done various things in life, but my really serious profession is teaching. Perhaps my poetry, too, is educational, like that of the old masters who wrote poems about medicinal herbs or curing mules? I think the answer is 'yes', but the subject of these lessons is basically myself: my joys and sorrows, beliefs and disappointments – and hopes, unexplained hopes.

Creation

This one's faulty, you observed, lifting me
from among the pieces arriving on
the conveyor belt with an unvarying rhythm.
You held me up to the light, scrutinising me
with expert, half-closed eyes, turned me
in your soft fingertips, squeezed me briefly
then gave me a tap with your fingernail, let
a drop of some acid or other fall on me
(this last, it must be admitted, with an air
of concentration, barely touching me
with your pipette). Everything was, however,
as it should be, colour, texture. You took
a sniff of me, but nothing wrong there either.
This one's faulty, you observed, putting me
back among the swarming finished products.

Family Photo Album

Of the numerous shots taken, not even one
showed father and son looking at each other,
far less smiling! The old guy merely smirked
now and again, from beneath mirror-coated
sunglasses. Despite being false, his teeth
looked the real thing, they were
so yellow from nicotine. The son never opened
his mouth, as if all it needed were
one last straw, the tiniest imaginable, and
he'd shout out loud: mouth gaping,
throat clenched, vomit back his genes
in the face of one he got eyes, throat
and teeth from, everything he had.

Angel in the Next Underground Coach

I'd look at you if I were sure you'd seen me.
Instead, I do my best to look elsewhere.
It's you, though. Doubt's enthroned there on your nape.
Your back is scrawny, like a grown-up's.

You stand in the next coach, turned half away.
You still cut your hair short. Your mouth is open.
We used to put our things in the same bag.
I'm scared of you. Workplace, a family.

Now I see you reflected in the doors.
In years gone by I had you all around.
I've got past you. Don't make me vanquish you.
No need for friendship. Better if I vanish.

You held me gently, understanding nothing,
Leaf from a tree, I fell onto your palm.
You knew it all, not knowing it was all.
You could lift me as a puppy gets lifted.

On the Big Dipper

Were I to pause, I'd have to sober up.
Better to look a fool, stark naked,
screaming and shrieking as it all spins round,
even if it's unseemly to get
so out of control. Like the day the big dipper
ground to a halt. The contraption had broken down.
Prosaically the mechanic clambered
along the rails, bawled at the people below.
We sat there through minutes, long enough
for it all to evaporate: the fear, the airy stomach.
The cut-price pleasure vanished, and left
only the narrow tracks reeking of oil,
nails, a light switch seen from an angle,
a dreary Hades, real life. No more bumping,
swooping. And I froze. No more tumbling,
or dizziness as you gasped to catch your breath.

Take Down his Particulars

Sweat's dripping from his nose
as he sniggers, jostles me, sniggers again
because I don't know his name. 'Want me to tell you?'
No need to bother, better to have him
chisel it into me, as a sculptor
leaves his imprint, impact after impact,
on the undressed marble. That's the way.
Darting about, the watery chisel
sends splinters flying, enters particulars
in amongst the marble's veins.
'Want to know my name then?' and he thrusts.
'No,' I gasp, 'please don't!' That makes him stop.
'Don't what?' 'Don't tell me!' Now he starts
to focus on the details, hair after hair,
inch after inch, uncovering the sculpture
that has lurked for so long in the marble.
Sweat's dripping from his nose,
it makes my eyes sting, there's no name for this,
no telling where, that's tough even for marble.
My God, dynamite! Sculpture and all, we explode.
Particulars swim off in every direction.

Better Staying Put

The thing I can't cope with is rushing on.
Such as: you fall asleep, then you wake up,
you fall in love, and then start hating them.
When guests are going to come, you stand around
in the shop not knowing what to do,
hoping to turn into a partygiver;
once they have left, the furniture needs to
be pushed back where it goes when you're alone.

That's when the going's tough. But staying put,
that's great! I'm a dab hand at being asleep
and being awake can give me lots of fun.
I'm happy when whole crowds come on a visit,

when someone loves me, and when no-one does.
But rushing from one state of things into
another state – that really puts me out.

I'd like to stay put till the end of time:
when I'm awake, to watch attentively
or, when I'm sleeping, dig a deeper pit;
dissolve the powdered soups of loneliness
or else sort through the mess my partner leaves.
What hurts is rushing. Slipping through the narrow
orifice of change leaves bruises later.

Silent Interval

The intervals were hard to tolerate,
reality caught up.
Provided you were working, things that needed
done swept you along, perspiring, happy:
I don't exist, I work.
All of a sudden, deafening silence,
no let-up of tension
in the cramped office. Just like a grounded
tightrope walker, everything so solid
it hurts. I'd need to sway
or else, to be immured in concrete, half
of a perfect couple whose afternoons
reek of cheese, enmeshed in relatives.
But as for me, I'm free!
Knowledge piles up without there being any
hope of ever reading your way through it:
your desk accuses you.
Time for a cup of tea, but the hotplate
gives no flicker of heat, maybe the cable
I came upon in a corner is faulty,
the one from pre-war days.
A half-hour break so long it drives you crazy,
just like a loaded gun.
Another one lies waiting far away,
unbending, prostrate. Cleverness's toll.

Better to bite one's nails. And learn lots more.
Lessons are sugar sweet.

Swaying Chandelier

The things we never speak of hang there in the room,
swaying like a chandelier someone knocked into
a moment ago, then scurried to hide behind
the furniture. Now from some undefined spot he
observes us observing the great, swaying taboo.

One of My Paintings

Icebergs piled on top of one another,
a crack unerringly straight, crystal-clear
water, post that's collected once a fortnight,
that's what I'd paint, visible exhalations,
a boat as it glides noiselessly across
a sluggish lake in the process of freezing,
black shadows in the contours of a gleaming
mountain range, a narrow highroad like
a plumb-line, still three hundred miles to go
before you come upon – no matter what.

Some Sort of Mirror at the End of the Room

The big room's an odd place to sleep in
when the wind whispers, the bed sighs
and your stomach coughs up lumps of food.
Look at him, fast asleep and sweating,
smiling, at peace, as devoid of sense
as the times in which we live. Some sort of mirror
at the end of the room; as we fall asleep,
drops of bitterness form on our lips.
No way of knowing what love is,
you can only tap it out or sing it,
sneeze it, or else let it choke you.

The basic questions, generalised grief
keep him and his generation busy,
but if the distress gets to cosmic levels,
life is still holding me in its arms.
What levels of thickness the skin attains!
How well we learn to tolerate each other!
Yet night after night he comes close to yelping,
his muscles tense in pursuit of a dream,
and his knees dig their imprint into my tummy.

Adam and Eve

The way Adam and Eve loved one another,
regal and yet somehow down to earth.
They had nobody else, for far and near,
where the devil was their like to be seen?

Sleep was the thing that gratified them most.
Adam's stench and Eve's grunting broadcast
far and wide news of their peace, their treasure.

The way Adam and Eve loved one another,
as creatures do, with no alternative.
Finding far off an edible root, each
called to the other: Why not try this too?

Sleep was the thing that gratified them most.
Adam's bristles, Eve's damp spots left them stuck
to one another like a shaving brush.

Adam and Eve, though, never loved each other.
It never crossed their minds what they were doing.
Love reflects on itself. Look, I'm like this,
you're like that, I, you, do it to each other.

It's pointless sleeping in a glorious stink,
a grunting shaving brush, unless you know
what you are doing. Loving needs a mirror.

Just Go!

This is how it will be: me standing on
the platform, with my suitcase in my hand,
while, darling, you are unable to reach me,
all you can do stand weeping on the platform
opposite, the railway lines, a fence
separating us. Your hands are thrust
into your pockets, otherwise you'd run
the risk of actually waving. Don't
give anything away, not now or ever,
every single eye is trained on us
and somewhere closed-circuit TV is watching.
It pulls in then, totally undistinguished,
crammed and filthy, uncomfortable,
here democracy still calls the shots.
I catch your eye: 'Just look now, I was right!'
You told me to go first-class, said you'd pay.
Thanks, it was kind, but I'll stick with the rest,
as you see, all the coaches are the same,
just go, don't stand and watch the train pull out.

Self-Portrait

Like a hamster scratching out a hole,
packing his swollen cheeks tight full of seeds,
always changing his mind, now here, now there,
fearful to see how little he's achieved,

but keeping busy. He prepares his litter,
dismantling it all the following day.
Night finds him where morning had left him. When
will it be finished? At his funeral?

Tampering here and fussing there, his litter's
changed each day, but still only half done.
Chaotic, yet it keeps him off the ground.
He lies down, twenty claws, a bag-shaped face.

Consuming lots of energy's the thing:
the light glitters in ripples on his fur.

All poems translated by Christopher Whyte

ANDRÉ NAFFIS-SAHELY is a poet, critic and translator. He was born in Venice to Italian and Iranian parents, and grew up in Abu Dhabi. He has a BA in History and Politics and an MLitt in Creative Writing from the University of St Andrews. His translations include Rashid Boudjedra's *The Barbary Figs* (Arabia, 2013), Abdellatif Laâbi's *The Bottom of the Jar* (Archipelago, 2013), and Émile Zola's *Money* (Penguin, forthcoming 2014).

These poems are either episodes from history or from the story of my life: episodes rescued, as Lowell once put it, from 'amnesia, ignorance and education'. The relentless pursuit of joy often distracts us from appreciating the magnitude of the moment as it occurs. Poetry rectifies that: it is the archaeology of such moments.

Blood and Proverbs

After four decades of early mornings and late nights,
Ferdowsi had completed his epic, the *Shahnameh*,
and so set out for the court of Sultan Mahmud,
who'd once promised him a gold piece per couplet;

Ferdowsi had written sixty thousand of them...
Unfortunately, Sultan Mahmud was uneasy:
he missed the gluey feel of blood on his hands,
and so sent the poet away with a mere sack of silver.

Years later, as the Sultan was about to ride into battle,
a minister recited a song of singular beauty;
and when the Sultan learned Ferdowsi was its author,

he sent Ferdowsi a caravan overladen with gold,
but as the caravan entered the city through one gate,
the poet's body was being wheeled out through the other.

Augury

They were dying, the Romans, and they knew it:
fewer sandals took to their roads, and wars
were getting pricier, bloodier, less satisfying too;

but once fear got a hold of the Romans,
it never released them. Their recourse was walls,
higher walls: the blind ecstasy of mortar and brick.

The more spirited ones threw lavish parties,
orgies – their spirits sinking as each of their guests
abandoned sinful pleasures for sanctity of the Cross.

Some blamed it all on the polluting barbarians
and so edicts were passed to outlaw the mixing of races.
Of all their flawed predictions, it was to be their last.

N16 8EA

It's comfortable here. The floors are soft
and up three flights there's a view;
the rent's not gone up in years and tomorrow

they're planting trees. If this paradise
were pocket-friendly, I'd take it anywhere –
but it isn't. Still, if I keep this patch

for some time, the postman might even
come to learn my name. How long will
my luck hold? If this were a casino

I would cash my chips in this instant,
but stability, it seems, is a dream that
you have in between one address and another.

This is where my love of roaming led me.

Family Business

He tore it down in a swoop,
your sweet loving Papa:
the Table of Elements
that watched over your sleep.

You were eighteen then, and
dissolving the scientist within
left the wall's whiteness unfilled,
turning its absence into a shrine.

That did it! A rebel on one day,
subjugated the morrow.
At least he was happy, your Papa,
he had found an apprentice

and left you footsteps to follow.
At parties and armed
with the deep angry wrinkles of learning,
he observed you, your Papa,

as you took to his trade:
which writers to flatter, which to ignore
and which to frown on benignly.
Yet the smile that you wore

was genuine somehow, beautiful even.
Now everyone knows you
kind Hannah Arnold,
who of course is the daughter

of the esteemed fearsome critic
Heinz Ludwig Arnold
... by the way tell me,
who is Heinz Ludwig Arnold?

Auroville

It was an enlightened apartheid: the spiritually
and materially liberated on one side,
and we barbarians on the other.

Imagine Indian mysticism spliced with
bad science-fiction films from the 60s: a giant
golden sphere on a manicured lawn,

and a few acolytes in the distance;
the off-limits distance. Vassals to the sun
busy scorching the red earth; we walked

through gardens tended by lean,
dark-chocolate Tamils: they hated their work
and they showed it, their disgruntled

demeanour piercing the tenuous peace.
We followed the signs back to the tourist centre
and decided on lunch. The café and shops,

which unlike the rest of the city were
open to all, might have been an IKEA store:
a kindergarten for the thrifty consumer,

rounded edges and colourful blandness.
Although Auroville residents made no use
of paper or coin currencies, we as outsiders

paid for our incense and scented soaps
with dirty rupees. Manufactured to subsidise
'Auroville's plans for a sustainable future',

their products are available online,
as well as in upmarket outlets in London,
Paris, Tokyo, New York and Berlin.

(near Puducherry)

Professional Vagabonds

Unlike the Mongols before them,
this is a horde that raises no dust,
and handles neither bullet nor sword;

theirs is a different sort of invasion:
one involving visa and suitcases
that slide neatly right under their seats.

No one city can claim them; every street
that they walk might as well be in Chicago,
Chennai, Taipei or Dubai. 'Geography'

is a word they often hear but consider
both vast and useless. What is life if not
brief glimpses of rivers, suburbs, of houses

they will never sit still in? Such thoughts
are best left to the nights and there are
not a few sleepless ones… This is a tribe

highly prone to nostalgia and familiar
to places like building sites, kitchens –
to stalls where the scrubbers of toilets

dream of old patients and stethoscopes.
In the land of their birth, each end
of the month is an occasion for a feast,

one bought by the cash which they wire
across mountains and oceans. Adaptable,
tireless, long-legged and peaceful – this

is a species whose turf covers the whole
of this brightly lit and bewildering world:
like the lichen, the mollusc, the killer whale,

or even the monarch butterfly – an insect
that mates and reproduces during its journey,
so that each larva always wakes in a land

both excitingly new and terrifyingly foreign,
and every successive generation carries on
with the next stage of their endless migration.

An Island of Strangers

The roof was the place to be. I was fifteen
and in love with ash-cans, pigeon coops,
women hanging their laundry. There was a fifty-
foot portrait of the King – always smiling –

by the sea, overlooking a busy junction;
like an ad for toothpaste or mouthwash.
At night, the shore on the west side of town
was the quietest, where hotels, *natashas* and *haram*

coalesced into parties. Every half-lit room
was a sure sign of orgasms and the passing
of money from stranger to stranger. Anything
interesting and pleasurable was *haram*. I envied

the King, and his sons, all eighteen of them.
The King was virile, a patriarch, Abraham on Viagra;
his people, on the other hand, were on Prozac.
Everywhere the eye looked was money; the nose,

meanwhile, hit only sweat: acrid, pugnacious, pervasive.
Most of the boys I knew sucked butane, smoked,
saved up for whores, waited for their parole in the summer.
Each back to their own country. Come September

the dissatisfied return; misfit mutts, at home every-
and nowhere. A friend compared cosmopolitanism
to being stuck at summer camp, to waiting for parents
who never showed up. In the twentieth year of his smile,

the King finally died. His mausoleum is a meringue: wavy,
white, empty… His sons have gone on squabbling, playing
'whose is biggest' with bricks; one by one, they die in car crashes…
Days of heat strokes, kif and bloodthirsty Ferraris.

The Journalist Speaks of the Dictator

I do not like the taste in my mouth.
To remonstrate would be better,
to keep my mouth shut would be best.
I can count – and know how many
lost their nerve at the sight of his smile
and how many more died in silence
sliding down the slick wall of his teeth.

The Return
for Alexandra

What city stays still like a glass-cased clock?
I wish this one did. I can't let it out of my sight:
the coffee-house I emptied my cup in one day

has turned into a beauty salon, and the houses
I once lived in are no longer there. All my life
I wanted to show someone this strange town,

and now that you're here I just sit by the creek
and mumble something incoherent in disbelief –
little to do except list the sights in a *Guinness*

Book of Records way, or explain how there were no
museums or libraries, no interesting ones anyway?
All that hate and here I am. Narrow wooden boats

sail past the bright hotels. This whole country
is like a hotel: a sweaty ride in a glass elevator;
at the ding of the doors, a chance to escape.

Forward March
for my grandfather

You were an odd sight: efficient and pasty-skinned
in the land of perpetual sunbathers. Your only talk
talk of dogs and money, their similar grease and stink.

You disliked the sea; love was an invisible coastline,
difficult, inaccessible. You preferred mountains:
Teutonic altitudes, dug-outs, old shells. You had one

overruling obsession, the war, the Second World War;
the one you missed out on: 'too young'. Unfazed
you brought it home, your own home. Your enemies:

your Hausfrau and two children. They, unlike soldiers,
were never allowed to surrender. Films on Rommel,
your hero, electrified your old frame. Somehow despite

having read his letters, you overlooked *Krieg ohne Hass*.
No quarter! When senility put you before its tribunal,
they offered you life (with limitations). You refused.

Exile, Italian Style
for my mother

Our family has become a government-in-exile;
visiting you is like paying my respects
to a kindly, downhearted minister who
is equally fearful of past, present and future.

Two small rooms to eat and sleep in; only
the essentials escaped being boxed up
while awaiting their destination. Still they wait.
This is home for now – a little town

outside Florence where the streets are empty
and the old stick their necks out of windows
like turtles keeping an eye out for vultures.
When apart, we speak only a little – two

talking heads in a penumbra chatting via a laptop.
I look at you: a Hausfrau without a Haus,
without a husband too. Pondering it all,
I chew anti-acids with a sovereign indifference …

Your younger son, your adjutant, or aide-de-camp,
shuts himself in his room all day and shoots aliens,
Nazis or terrorists on his console – almost
as if training for a war to reconquer our lives.

VIVEK NARAYANAN was born in India to Tamil-speaking parents and grew up in Zambia. He did undergraduate and graduate work in the United States, taught at the University of KwaZulu-Natal in Durban, South Africa, and moved back to India in 2000. His first book, *Universal Beach*, was published in Mumbai in 2006 (Harbour Line) and released in a second US edition (Ingirum Books) in 2011. His second book of poems, *Life and Times of Mr S*, was published in New Delhi by HarperCollins in 2012. He is co-editor of the India-based journal and literary publisher, *Almost Island.*

The Jewelled Deer, excerpted here, is, in its early stages, a sequence spun out from specific passages in Valmiki's *Ramayana*. This is the earliest Sanskrit version, a text quite different from the more devotional story that most Indians have in their heads. I am working mainly from two scholarly, annotated prose translations, and also drawing on a reading of the many different waves of Sanskrit poetry. In the Sanskrit tradition, Valmiki is referred to as the *Aadikavi* ('first, or foundational poet'); yet the *Ramayana* today is most often understood more as story, or worse, as history. One of my aims is to try to reanimate the *Ramayana* as poem; there is not a single viable verse translation currently extant in English.

My method for this is open and evolving. The grammatical/linguistic, metrical, psychological and aesthetic distance between the trigger text and our understanding of poetry in English today may well be too great to allow for anything remotely like a straightforwardly 'faithful' translation, except as academic exercise. This is a potentially exciting problem, providing that the contemporary poet still writes herself *through* the features, textures and narrative contradictions of the original rather than simply bypassing them altogether.

At the moment, by focusing on specific passages and fragments, I can partly set the larger narrative aside (interested readers would already know it, or get it in unreliable flashes or look it up elsewhere) and aim for a more kaleidoscopic, intensified effect; also one that sometimes makes use of contradictions to run against the thrust of the original. Working in fragments allows me to draw on a variety of approaches and be open to the full range of formal resources available in English today.

Rama

Rama   hero with hair dark as a crow's wing
        Your son is not your son
Rama   hero still with the curling sidelocks
        Your son is not your son
Rama   hero of the heavy lotus eyes
        Your son is not your son
Rama   speechless and radiant with swords
        Your son is not your son
Rama   tiger among men
        Your son is not your son
Rama   blank face turned to the face of Saturn
        Your son is not your son
Rama   who will never grow sick or tired
        Your son is not your son
Rama   three-headed cobra from behind
        Your son is not your son
Rama   forest tangled in the heart
        Your son is not your son
Rama   sip of clearer water
        Your son is not your son
Rama   empty gaping dark
        Your son is not your son
Rama   corpse within the corpse
        Your son is not your son
Rama   your nipple in the rain
        Your son is not your son
Rama   sleep beyond all sleep
        Your son is not your son

Tataka

Sage, tell me, who is she, this
disfigured one with the rage
and force of a thousand
elephants? How does
a woman come to be this strong
that whole armies
crossing into her forest are simply torn
to strips of skin and lumps
of rotting, half-chewed flesh?

        Rama, she is Tataka,
once the most beautiful and tender woman
in the world, jewel of a daughter
to the virtuous and powerful Suketu,
wife to the gentle Sunda,
mother of the fearless Maricha.
It happens that her husband
was killed and
she and her son cursed
with these, the
hideous forms you see.
Now she hates Agastya and all of us
with every drop of her being.

Sage, who killed her husband Sunda?
Who disfigured Tataka's body?

Rama, you must never hesitate
to kill a woman, not
for a second. This is the immortal unwavering
rule for men charged with the burden of kingship.

Rama's Servants

Punisher bladed discus	Dharma bladed discus	Kaala bladed discus
Vishnu's bladed discus	Indra's bladed discus	Vajra h-bomb
Siva's lance	Brahma's Crest	Aishika guided missile
Brahma's artillery	Time's wrench	The Tower
noose of Dharma	noose of Kala	noose of chemical rain
The Drier	The Drencher	Pinakin's ballistic missile
Agni's long-range fire-thrower	Vayu's air-to-air missile	The Drainer
The Horse-head missile	Vilaapana bomb	The Wrester
Kankila machine	The Peacemaker	Kaapaala sniper rifle
Mohana poison gas	Kankana assault rifle	Taamasa cruise missile
Nandana gilded sword	Saumana tactical missile	Varunastra heavy-weight torpedo
Maanava anti-tank missile	Brah-mos II hyper-sonic missile	Prasvapana anti-ship missile
Sudarshan laser-guided bomb	Saura thermobaric bomb	Maayaadhana cluster bomb
Nirbhay subsonic missile	The Dispossessor	The Cooler
Tvastr's deadly Sudaamana	Prithvi short-range ballistic missile	Agni intercontinental missile
Sagarika submarine-launched missile	Raudra rocket launcher	Aindra sub-machine gun
Paasupata interceptor missile	Gaandharva fire bomb	Dhanush anti-ballistic missile
The Yawner	The Humidifier	Vidhwansak anti-material rifle
Aakash surface-to-air missile	Brahma's cordon	The Monster
Vaayavya artificial weather machine	Shivalik multi-grenade launcher	Shaurya glide missile

Calling his servants in, Rama
caressed their heads, their
shoulders, their
curves and knobs, blowing
lightly on their deadliest
points, their sharp
mouths, licking
lightly the thought

of bodies with the last
force crackling
out of them; and when
as Rama's loyal
servants they drew
close letting themselves
be touched and touched so,
he closed
his eyes
whispered:

form into name into kill

What the People Said
(upon hearing of Rama and Lakshmana's departure for the forest)

'My god, even with sandal paste, the forest will totally ruin Sita's complexion.'

*

'Oh Rama, such a sweetheart!'

*

'Rama, we will leave all our belongings for you!'

*

'Rama, we will burn ourselves alive for you!'

*

'Ah, those royal thugs, let them suffer. What do they know of pain?'

*

'I think it's a good thing. A king should always know his foreign policy.'

*

'Well, I suppose Bharatha will be screwing Rama's other wives then.'

*

'So what's with Lakshmana? Are they a threesome?'

*

'See that? The entire state apparatus has just come to a grinding halt, life goes on.'

*

'Rama always obeys his parents. Why can't you?'

*

'I'm thirsty just for the sight of them.'

*

'O Rama, Sita, the world seems missing when you're gone.'

Chitrakuta

And to that mountain paradise set on fire
by the red blossoms of the kimsuka tree,
the honeycombs hanging like buckets,
the marking-nut trees, the cry of the moorhen,
the bleat of the peacock, the herds
of elephants and the echoing birds,
they arrived with open eyes. Sita
gathered firewood and fruit while the brothers
caught and killed some quick deer, rabbit,
wild fowl. Famished, they ate on the riverbank.

The next day readying for the long darkness
to come, Lakshmana sacrificed a black antelope
with a splotch of red on its forehead.
Arrows removed, bleeding stanched, the animal
was gently strangled then laid down
with its legs pointing North, then stroked
and pleasured, washed in all the openings
by which its life-spirit had fled: mouth, nose,
eyes, ears, navel, penis, anus, hooves.

In the beginning, the gods accepted man
as victim. Later, the ability to be sacrificed
passed into antelope and horse;
from horse into cattle, from cattle
into sheep, from sheep into goat, then from
goats into the earth, so all the world
was touched by our humility, our
complicity. Outside the leaf-thatched hut,
the animal was raised on a spit and roasted
until it had attained a deep, dark brown colour.
Chanting the appropriate verses, taking care
not to break the bones, Rama carved the animal
limb by limb, cut by cut, setting aside the grain
of its hair, the flour of its skin, taking into him only
the dough of its flesh, the sublime fat of its marrow.

The Jewelled Deer

Gathering in all his powers,
every ounce of himself, Maricha
turned into a deer:
                                        face
mottled dark and light,
blue and pink, alert ears like
sapphires, neck gently elongated,
belly glowing like the moon,
sides soft like the pale velvet
of the mahua flower,
slim, slender legs,
tail tinged with all the
colours of the rainbow. And in
his skin studded everywhere with
diamonds and precious stones,
he was both utterly deer-like
and unlike any deer that
had ever been seen.
                        So with little
deer bleats he flickered
in and out of the trees, made
his way to the grove where Sita,
golden-skinned herself, plucked
flowers.
              In the clearing he shone
with a sudden brightness that hurt
the eyes. Some of the other animals
neared him, sniffed, then quickly
bolted. Hunter now turned
to prey, he kept his calm.
                              Completely still as he
was, it took a while for Sita's eyes
to find him but when they did
she dropped her half-made garland and stared
a long minute in awe. Then greed –
or equally just a hopeless yearning to be
fulfilled – took possession of her.
'Rama, that gleaming deer,
nibbling at tender shoots, I must
have him! Whether as pet or

plaything, he would look so good
in our hut. Aren't we already
visited by herds of yak and spotted
antelope, apes, monkeys and
kinnaras of all kinds? And when
it's time to go home
we can take him with us!
He'll be the pleasure
of the palace girls. Just don't say no.
Bring him alive if you can but if you
have to kill him I should still like his skin
stretched over a cushion of straw,
it would make such a pretty seat!'
                              Rama and
Lakshmana stared at the wonder
glowing in the shadows like
the hare-marked moon.
'Rama,' said Lakshmana,
'That deer can't be real.'
They watched the quick darts
of its flame-like tongue:
flashes of lightning in a cloud.
'So what if it isn't, Lakshmana,
for centuries we have claimed
the beasts of the forest as ours. I'll
kill it for meat. And if it's Maricha
in disguise, I'll kill it anyway.
He deserves to die.'
                              Saying this Rama resolved
to go in pursuit, but at the very
moment he had done
so, the deer disappeared. Following
the sounds of crushed twigs
and leaves, sighting it
in sudden flares of light, leaping
to rival the sun, now close, now
far, now seen, now not, now a leg,
now a diamond tip of
horn, now a band of tail. Driven
half-insane, Rama hurled
himself at those woods. Then
spotting it in a shady

nook of the meadow unaware, he
drew his bow with the triple curve
and shot a flaming arrow that glared
towards it like a snake. The arrow
found its mark. The deer leaped
in the air, took two steps then
stumbled, then regaining its
feet, bleeding a red line
from its side, stumbled again
and dragged itself away while he
showered three more
thin arrows, one of them piercing
the neck. With a high-pitched bark
the animal fell
to the grass. Immense pain;
Maricha was beginning to feel his true
form coming back, his massive torso,
his two long fangs, his dark
body, the glistening gold
of earring and necklace.
But before this had become
completely apparent, Rama felt
a strange moment of recognition
when the dying deer screamed,
'Oh Sita! Oh Lakshmana!
How will Sita react to this?
Great-armed Lakshmana, what will he think?'
Then the faint recognition curdled
to fear, pangs of outright
terror rising in spasms, left
eye twitching: the deer
had spoken those words in Rama's
own voice. Unable to shake or make
sense of or forget or even put
his mind off what this meant,
Rama killed a second deer
and carrying the meat hurriedly
retraced his steps to Janasthana.

LEONIE RUSHFORTH has published poems in a range of journals and magazines and won the Keats-Shelley Prize in 2003. She chaired the Forward Poetry Prizes panel in 2012. She is a teacher of English at St Paul's Girls' School and lives in London.

It's appropriate that the first poem in this group, 'How To Get There', is a set of directions; writing a poem is usually a process of making my way somewhere I can't get to using normal navigational instruments like thought or conversation. Most of these poems are linked with specific places: the Freud Museum in Hampstead regularly hosts exhibitions and recently showed the work of Louise Bourgeois – the extraordinary *Janus Fleuri* was one of the pieces in that show; Fontenay is a twelfth-century Cistercian abbey in Burgundy, intact, much visited; Gorky Park, at the time this poem was written, was still the park planned by the constructivist architect Melnikov in 1928. Two other poems need a brief note: 'Song for Carmen' was previously published in the December/January 2003 issue of the *London Magazine*; 'You With Work To Do' is a version of Pushkin's poem 'The Prophet'.

How to Get There

The derelict tavern marks the turn. Follow the lane
narrowing all the while and bordered by tall dark trees,
light-eating conifers, and wonder where the village
begins as the bends conduct you through the fields on the
low road, banks rising on either side, and feel relief
when the church emerges set back on your left, flanked by
the rectory and the modest church room where you find
four elderly people finishing a meeting who
compete to explain the one thing you already know,
the graveyard is not the cemetery, not at all, and
that to find the dissenters you must take the Duddery
all the way to the small crossroads and not (as you did
and have been rueing this long morning) accept the first
invitation that appeared to speak to memory
but led in a wide and empty circle back to the
boarded windows of the tavern – but go on, go on
to the crossroads, to the edge of what still can't rightly
be called a village and turn left past over-tended
houses where willow fencing and pink paint confect a
rural fantasy to find yourself at what will turn
out to have been Meeting Green though there will be no sign
and soon again another turning you'll resist to
the left which leads away from what has never really
happened towards the rise and half way up, pull over;
park on the verge; step out and to the iron gate secured
by a string easily slipped. Let it swing back. Scan the
windy field. Try to remember where it is and why
you can't remember your way back to the small flat slab,
back to the shock of his name.

On the Ource

The oars are keeping time, a touch
of blade to the clear body of water's enough
to change course, send the boat
towards the bank or under grey ash arms
into a tangle of italic leaves –

so drift on a cold current further down
to the little weir and the pool below
where white cattle dip their heads
and the long bridge lopes its easy arches
over the heron's back and bleaching grass.

Let go. Let the ticking minutes slowly sink.
The oars are shipped, last sound, and out of silence
skimming faster than eyes can tell the mind
to see the kingfisher hurls its *blue*

over the drifting boat where I hold tight,
in the ash trees' shade, knuckles gleaming.

Janus Fleuri *at the Freud Museum*

The stillness is a spell. How can such a weight float
like that above the couch? How it makes apparent
the inscrutability of symmetry, its requiring of nothing. The
                                                    bronze
gleams softly in the little light. It is not a play.
It is not a response. The breast is the phallus is the breast is the
                                                    phallus.
Tender and absolute they have cancelled time, determined all
confession. There is no need to look at anything else.
Questions confirm their serene tyranny, the silent assumption
of all the nerves' thrillings to the world. This doubleness a single
gate you will always be passing through.

Kairos
for Heather

Late October and long shadows on the beach where
bathers recline under fraying coconut shades
and swipe always too slowly at the sand flies
with a Kindle or Kermode's *The Sense of an Ending*,

not quite not there,
bodies aware of the pulse of the sun,
the small kisses of the persistent flies
and the Russian women in peripheral

vision who knit a conversation across
little distances, one seated on a rock smoking,
a second wrapping thin arms around
herself on her towel, the comfortable third

in her straw hat paddling in the idle waves,
not quite lost in the fictions and the theories
of the fictions, and tuning in to the heavy heart
that seems to be slowing to a standstill

in anticipation of the flock of pigeons that skims
in over their shoulders, low and fast,
as the fish leap in a shower of commas
out beyond the buoy and suddenly

purple grey clouds have docked and are pushing
down on the empty café, the sunbeds,
the young father holding his shining baby
who screams in delight or fear above the lucid water.

Fontenay

one of us can be seen running in slow motion
waving like a man in a memory

in a suddenly meaningful sunlight
towards the dark gateway where the rest of us wait

the children's upturned faces gleam like moons
pale   pulled close in to the planetary gravities

of plaintive parents longing to saunter
into the heat down gravel paths   to be dwarfed

in the austerity of the aisle
reach the cloister intact   the children cluster

•

in the church a cold child holds his mother's cloak
cradled in her smile's horizon   an idea

to warm the chill of a communal cell
coherent celibate lives   the aisle is earth

(one of us crouches low   mimes rolling boules)
and leads to a retable where in damaged relief

a pre-revolutionary ox absent-mindedly
eats a baby in a manger   *Death's Door* is open

behind Our Lady   two of us stand carefully here
under the keystone   between the light and the shadow

•

one of us is piping the children
round the sweltering garden where a stranger

will tell them *you'll all go to hell*   swallows
are nesting in the pink ribs of the scriptorium

writing their tireless lines in and out of
the bright door   folding themselves up into nothing

over the lip of the cup of the nest
to feed their safely panic-stricken young

•

four of us have abstracted themselves
celebrate with illuminated smiles

and upturned faces their *unity*
with the rigorous lines laid down by the authorities

for an hour   recreating childlessness
some of us are celibate   some of us worship mothers

•

one of us has found his daughter again
he has taken her to look at trout

milling slowly in *the famous hatchery*   fat as monks
who sold the abbey off to Monsieur Hugot

fast when Jacobin fires flickered too close
the forge   *a veritable factory*

is dead   long live the hydraulic hammer
they invented here   in the most beautiful room

•

two of us linger blithely   knowing
they won't be left behind   while

in the car park the children catapult
themselves into their parents and yelling like devils

ricochet off to guillotine ants
with the picnic knife in the long last hours

of an adults' afternoon
running in slow motion to next year's seed

Mist Lifting on Mount Caburn
for Shirley

The valley is somewhere behind us inside
the mist as we are, as everything is this
November morning of extrapolating

another way, of going on without you,
and the mist is making clear what that is
already like, the way we are having to

trust the upward slope to take care of us, to
pay attention to the smallest closest things
at our feet, for example the toppling

tiny black and white snails in the challenges
of the wet grass, the absence of sound except
breath, the way a bench forms itself out of the

paleness and suggests we sit ourselves down for
a moment when the mist begins to admit
our eyes and we sit in a row and take stock.

The membrane thins to a yellow glow, darkens
to a hillside, and we have never waited
with such confidence, looked so intently as

at this emerging grassland, the diagram
trees and thorns, the run of railway cottages,
the maggot train trundling its minutes, the farms,

or wondered as at this confirmation of
faithful effort in the human map below,
the whole clear unmiraculous valley. We

squint up at the ridge where the red cattle burn
gold, turn our backs on the bones at the distant
summit we don't need to reach.

Gorky Park

in Gorky Park
the sky was high
and blue, the crowds
we walked among
were nothing like
the crowds we knew

on shady gravel
paths we wandered
through a pleasure
ground whose numbered
days turned
round slow

spellbound, measured by
the stately ferris
wheel we rode
above the soviet
city and its river
into silver air

and down, to watch
our emptied seats
rising to the view
again accompanied
by the distant sound
of fiddles, the notes

of a folk dance
leaping and falling
through the still
unfolding leaves

Song for Carmen

Alabaster blossom in the orange groves.
The evening sways in the sweetness

as the sun sets behind the shoulder of the hill
and four dogs leave the village, bound for Melegis

where dusk will meet them. Now Orion
surfaces in deepening blue; children on doorsteps

count his belt's three stars and when
two women turn that corner by the church

it is dark. The steeply rising street is a white spine
leading to the square where someone sits

alone, smoking. The moon takes
a silver bar and prises open

Carmen's window to disclose
her room wreathed in the perfume of the trees,

the perfect linen of her empty bed.
The hillside sighs. Staring in, the moon forgets

itself a moment – then slides away to Senegal.

You With Work To Do
after Pushkin

The city streets were dark and empty. I was tired
and half way home and stood irresolute
at the cross-roads when what I must call an angel
appeared beside me at the kerb. She touched my eyes
with light fingers and I stared into the world
like a frightened eagle. She touched my ears and filled
them with ringing sound: and I heard the sky shudder,
the rush of thought, the slither of returning eels
in the muddy Thames, the leaves of the plane trees
unfolding. And she touched my lips and tore out
my lying tongue with its idle eloquence
and with a bloody hand she forced the biting wisdom
of the snake into my empty mouth. And she split
my body open with her sword and removed
my palpitating heart and she placed a flaming coal
where it had been. I lay on the wet pavement
like a dead woman and I heard a voice speaking
to me. It said: *Get up, you with work to do.*
                                   Bear witness.
                                   Listen.
                                   Be filled with purpose.
                                   Cross continents and oceans.
                                   Sear people's hearts with words.

KERRIN P. SHARPE was born in Wellington, New Zealand, and now lives in Christchurch, teaching creative writing at the Hagley Writers' Institute. Her first collection of poetry, *Three Days in a Wishing Well*, was published by Victoria University Press in 2012. Some of these poems have appeared in *Turbine, Best New Zealand Poems, Sport* and *TAKAHE*.

An early morning encounter with a deer's head impaled on a school fence, and then imagining the opportunity to put the same deer back in his rightful environment, gave rise to the poem 'a possible journey'. Though we never spoke a word, the experience of sitting next to an orthopaedic surgeon on a plane resulted in 'six lies for an orthopaedic surgeon'. I actually saw a man cleaning a wishing well and suddenly wishes seemed no longer private. As well as meetings and sightings, I like to write about memory and invent it. Artworks are particularly inspiring; so are birds and animals and the world of science. I enjoy making connections with words that open the door to the imagination, and the juxtaposition of the unlikely. This strangeness compels me to write.

a possible journey

the deer believes
words are enclosures

even weather forecasts
with their ridges

of high pressure
make wire fences

from the bambi
school of music

the deer watches
soccer crooning

chase chase with a
grey industrial tongue

he prefers the art
of tree grafting

eating raw apples
the rattle of stars

sewing the world

my mother's head
was full of stitches
she waited in the
deep forest as featherstitch
with other small birds

here she sang *rickrack* and
braided herring bone rivers
here she used chain stitch to
grow mountains here she sat
weaving stitch wheel oceans
to roll out waves

but there are white gaps
between smocking pirie street
and the cross-stitched church
where she married

if I follow the
red wool down woodward
street it appears as
running stitch in the
napier earthquake

her hat shops are only
tacked to pavements there
is a ladder watching
her needles unsure of
what she remembered

the tram goes home alone

six lies for an orthopaedic surgeon

I

he sat in the
ribcage of a plane
and studied a
parisian church
made of monk bones

II

after eating an apple
he felt like he had
taken an axe to a skull

III

in the great depression
his parents had to
hire bones from the
butcher to make soup
he recalls lifting
the lid off the copper pot
and seeing his first femur

IV

he chanted the
206 bones
in the human skeleton
like a rosary…
ulna fibula tibia

V

he showed his twins
maxilla and clavicle
how to remove bones
from their pet goldfish
while it was swimming

VI

when he spoke at the
conference only
the bones of 300
surgeons were listening

The Alchemy of Snow

Snow is often found
at the Biology bar
in the company of
potash and potassium.

*

Her different melting points
make relationships
difficult.

*

She can be driven.

*

She has many names:
Cyril, Tim, Bunny, Poppy
and so on. They form
the scaffolding of her
memory.

*

She is the fortunate
symbol of news from abroad
and appears in teacups.

*

The Edmonds book (1955)
published her recipes: Coconut
Ice, Vanilla Snow, Snow
Pudding and Melting Moments.

*

Using the Chatelier
Principle, she reverses
herself. There is this fruity smell.

*

Late at night farmers often
hear her playing the
accordion while she treats
psoriasis in their horses.

*

She is energy favourable.
For the painting *A Dutch Funeral*
snow slid a simple pine coffin
over frozen fields and under the
smock mill's criss-cross sails
and rickety gallery. She
decorated the black veils
of mourners and comforted
a small dog.

*

She is utterly faithful
to the blackbird.

three days in a wishing well

at the bottom
of the well
lined with porteous
yellow blue art tiles

ceramic hands hold
moon drop coins
arranged as feathers
on a hunter's shirt

and a city care
man with hose and
bucket is separating
wishes from water

the research is called
three days in a wishing
well now the council knows
the thoughts of the boy

rowing nowhere the
woman carrying shortbread
as live environments.com
even the washing

instructions for this poem

world without maps

on the margins of the world
monks raise farm animals

furrow remains indicate
a popular devotion

to beeswax figures
some still sketch

british birds and their eggs
or visit the sewing shrine

home of the bobbin
and cotton brothers

j & p coats
they are a silent order

so often singing is only
heard from the wine glass

or its reflection

because my father

because my father
taught me to draw rain

I cannot tell
if there are wings
behind my eyes
or the weight of words

sometimes I call
0800 angel
to hear the voice
of my son

and dig up his medicine
smaller than usual
buried in snow something
in the field reminds me

there was never enough

In the cart

My mother is standing on the little tooth wheel of the pie cart.
She has been warned never to visit houses on wheels, never to
associate with brown paper bags.

The pie cart wears a mourning cap. He raises it to the hearse. He
raises it to the trade waste he traps. He is full of respect. When he
asks *short or sweet,* he means pastry. The fluted kind. Black birds
sing to his pies.

The pie cart shows my mother how to make meat go further. He
shows her how to slip an eggcup under a blanket of pastry and
make a rosette.

My mother unpins her hat.

the rice planters 1953

on the steep stone path
to the rice shrine

the tea-bag horse
stops often to turn
the kettle on

his master removes
a straw jacket
to climb a tiny tree

this whistling bachelor
reminds the ikebana
rice planters the slow

moon will cross their palms
with the shadows
of pale fish

the whistler

combines fictional time with real time
a kind of psychic distance
a place that disappears

he remembers the whistle
of his father's liturgical comb
the personal address whistle
of his sermons that low whistle
from the bedside of the deceased

the excuse-for-work whistle
the stay-at-home whistle
the whistle that sweeps and cleans
an ancestral grave orientates
the whistler's intention

because they were born strangers
the whistler's children carry a gene
that allows them to stand on the street
and shake hands with someone upstairs

the whistler can be heard in far-off lands
he whistles his jacket back
from an argument in Samarkand

their faces turn pages

the beachcomber
keeps a button box

a cross section
of folded years

the anchor button
the immigrant button

the faithful button
of lighthouses

after the storm
the searchlight button

joins the button of silence
a roll call

for the dead button
of birds and fish

ta ka he
ta ka kau
ta ka ruha

there are few sightings

any man who has spent
an hour in the sea's gills
is a marine expert

the prediction of tides
and their stable doors

the saint's coffin
asleep on the seabed

the sea horse
of st cuthbert's gospel
are miraculous

unusual incidents
like forgetting

belong to the mute
who stopped speaking

long before his mother

IAN STEPHEN was born in Stornoway, Isle of Lewis and lives there still. His first book of poems, *Malin, Hebrides, Minches* was published by Dangaroo Press, Denmark (1983) and his most recent, *Adrift*, by Periplum, Czech Republic (1997). Other collections have appeared in Edinburgh, Scotland, with Morning Star and Polygon. His sequence of lyrics celebrating the archipelago of St Kilda, along with the music of David P. Graham, is due from Inventio-Musikverlag, Berlin, in 2013.

When I began to publish poems, in periodicals in different countries, around 1979, I was also taking part in performances. I read poems or told stories. These two strands have remained main interests although I also work in several other disciplines – as a playwright, a writer of fiction and non-fiction and as a visual artist, for example.

The more I'm immersed in telling stories – an improvised form where the audience plays a part in the mood and detail around a narrative – the more I feel that the opportunities of poetry are different. For me, the backbone of a story needs to be very clearly defined, before I can tell it. Like a voyage at sea, the route will never be exactly the same because the sea-conditions will be different. But there is a preconceived plan, open to alteration if conditions change.

In contrast, for me, poems are acts of discovery. I remember the artist Graham Rich being surprised when he saw words in my sketchbook. 'I thought you were drawing,' he said. But I was. In words, rather than line.

I used to take many photographs, nearly always in colour, first in slow Kodachrome and later with a digital camera. Sometimes I linked images to words, sharing the load between the two media. But in the last few years I've usually been working with language, spoken or written. I've completed a novel and I'm working on a book of personal voyages which have taken me through the startling imagery from traditional stories, both real landscapes and imagined ones.

This work has increased rather than decreased my interest in making poems. But I may have less need to tell a story within the recent poems. These might take the form of text-messages or they may be lyrics for a libretto. But I think I'm still drawing with the words, hoping to find something beyond what I'm seeing, while observing a particular thing in the world.

In Breton

In Breton, they say
there's a word that weaves between
green and blue, allowing for
haze, precipitation,
the burr of distance,
the welcome shock
of escaping light
warming your shoulders.

In Brest

Grey stones from Kersanton.
Ochre from Logonna. This is
a 1761 home
with its fountain watered again
in 1992.

Thanks mayor,
native of Recouvrance.
And for the cross on the gable,
part of a cemetery for the drowned.

But was it for the lost remains,
the recovered,
or both?

Che Perig et Anna

Lisa speaks in Fair Isle twang.
Perig speaks from inside the mind.

The song of this open house
is significant flexing
of original stairs.

Conversation on Ouessant

Our conversation rang
among the wary blasts
of restricted vessels
nosing fog
outside the marquee.

We drew our own charts,
ink on napkins.
We sipped red bread.
The telling blot
developing from spill.

I know that nobody's
scared of nothing.

I heard a story in translation –
how they used to sink
a big bell
down between the reefs
so a signal could be sent
under storm-water.
Long before
warning booms
were sustained
by gas.

Blue Woman, Brittany

Speaking as a navigator
guessing between
a prile of tidal periods
I can understand
in retrospect
now that my hull's been released
everything but
the suddenness.

Even the Mull, the
North Channel,
streams south of Arklow,
St George's Channel,
all allow
a grace of slack.

But I remember
3 hours into the passage
warning whorls at the Sound of Shiants
where the blue men hold the ship
and test the eloquence of all aboard.
And if they're satisfied they slack their grasp.

Even the skipper
has difficulty
responding
to the freedom of a sea
that starts to seem
too large.

Crossing the Minch

Enough light now
to show the shapes of waves,
the far run of big hills.

We can be caught
by individual traits
in particular clouds

as all these reds
are streaked by
electrical activity.

You are the goddess
of cumulonimbus
and I could be fascinated again

as the shadow of wit is across your eyes
and I know there's something like calm in your centre
but I'm also seeing the scud of dark
and know to get all vulnerable sail
to the deck fast and
brace before the sent ice hurts

and then I'll rub my unprotected ears and nose and eyes
and blink at yet another change of sky
and know that continuation would take
the bravery of the solo sailor in
an area of geos and williewaws
where the notes of pilotage
are sketchy.

But I'm on the ferry
and there's snow on *an Teallach*
and brightness on the *Coigeach* stone.

It could be time
for an egg-roll.

A way of putting things aside

There's a way of putting things aside
things that you'll need
or need to keep in case you do –

the falls from blocks
rove to advantage,
handy in a loose chain

and the top-rope,
the endless loop that keeps you safe –
that too is not coiled

but the hitches flow into each other
and they can't lock so
one pull and
the doubled lines
do fall.

There's pleasure in skill,
pleasure in seeing
how a thumb and two bent finger tops
hold the runs of rope.

It's intimate opera,
on deck or on the wall.

Sailmaker's whipping

Drawing on the backs of envelopes
which contain business
we should be dealing with
but
since we're here
the issue is the transfer
of the method of making
a sailmaker's whipping
from 3 strand cordage to
multiplait polyester.

The thread is waxed with finger-ends.
You get a grip on
the flat of the needle.

Did you know that the Breasclete smith
who took iron out to
the construction of
Flannan Isles light
made his own needle
when they were stranded
so the men could keep
their arses in their trousers?

It's techniques that save us
from the cold.
So don't call this
displacement.
That's something else again.

Cape Farewell – Scottish islands voyage
(text messages from *Song of the Whale*)

1 Clisham

the Harris bus is short
pensioners banter
long in the tooth
not a claw to be seen
but my mother said
you'd often see a goose
on a seat
as the gear got a grasp
of the side of Clisham

2 Balranald

eyebright and kidney vetch
but it's ladies' vetch
that thickens milk
by rye and bere and
cousins of buntings

dulse dulls in dry warmth
it will shine maroon in broth
as residue of other
seaweed tribes
filters to ragworm
and in turn
to dunlin

3 Lochmaddy

cats' paws
come quietly close
spinning bangles of spray
delicate until
the punching pressure
rocks us
not like a baby

4 St Kilda archipelago

it's a particular three
individual spears
dipping and trimming in nearly
mutual response to airs

and in present documented light
two islands of a known group
are bare to
their midriff rock

but you know they possess
summits somewhere
in the drizzle
and a whole neighbour
still concealed

5 Monach Islands

Ceann Iar

machair spills
a rough greening
to the sandline

this is where sea
gets eroded
but kicks back
on the other side

repels
falling boulders
tosses them
like pups
a long way in

Ceann Ear

the harling's gone so
you see the join –
bricks over stone

maybe one shift of scale
was enough –
market, catch or temperature

improvements crumble

will most of our developments
look like this
accidental balance?

the trapped fall and jamming
of three chimney stones

a still dance
without people

6   Taransay – wrecked trimaran revisited
do dh' Eoghann MacRath *(nach maireann)*

fraying loose ends
of glass cloth

dimples from lost
fastenings

copper stitches
delaminating ply

our stainless technology
– fast up
this tidal creek
– no paddles

lichens have a grip
– harmonic verdigris

a weft of salt
settled in
terrain
like *feannagan**

but songs have gone
from Tarasaigh
unless we
sing them now

* lazy-beds

TOH HSIEN MIN (b. 1975) has three published poetry collections, most recently *Means To An End* (2008). His work has also appeared in *Acumen, London Magazine* and the *London Review of Books*. He is a past president of the Oxford University Poetry Society and founder of the *Quarterly Literary Review Singapore*.

I write poetry with an instinct towards form. These poems set off in a new direction by exploring the line break unarmed with the more quantitative rules that characterise much of my other work.

'At night's border with the next day' breaks from the long-lined conversational cadence of my most recent collection, *Means To An End*. I'm a night person, most productive around midnight, and I don't think of it at all as the close of a day. These night crossings therefore take place imperceptibly, like differences that add up and only become apparent over a longer time horizon. The paradox is that it becomes less possible to know the past accurately after some distance of time.

'Quince' takes this further in tackling the mystery of beginnings. Our experience is cumulative, mathematically *continue à droite, limite à gauche*; but where exactly is that left bound? This informs the structure of the poem, where the left and right half-lines never meet until the end, which nevertheless is open to interpretation. The broken lines of 'Quince' take inspiration from Old English alliterative verse, albeit with the relaxation of requiring only one word on either side to match. In this way, the poem peers back into its own origins even as we use it to peer back into ours.

The alliterative form might sound challenging but it was easier to work with than the form in 'Airborne', where the weight of each line and sub-line had to be tested constantly. This difficulty in 'Airborne' was offset by the clarity of its purpose and narrative arc. The incidents in the poem occurred on separate flights in the same month. A couple of months prior to that, I had learned of the passing of the Filipino poet Sid Gómez Hildawa from pneumonia. Sid had been the most exciting poet to emerge from his country in the new millennium, and a warm and generous friend besides. I wanted to write a poem in his memory, and 'Airborne' was the result.

At night's border with the next day

At night's border with the next day
I think of becoming a different person
the way a tongue changes
with the crossing of a river
or the type of wheat.
It is the start of a new country.
There are new weeds to dig up.
The coming of storm is predicted
by other means. The light here
differs from the light of the old,
and in that light the actions of the past
seem to be monuments whose stone
is textured away by wind and rain.
Moss will set in, before it too dies,
as sand submerges granite
like a change of tides. In time,
the city will become uncertain.
Only archaeological speculation
on what sort of a civilisation
had lived here would thrive,
and if it fled because of famine
or was wiped out by disease
or conquered by complacency,
none will know. At that point,
there will be another night,
another border to cross.

Quince

The fruit that took Eve and Adam

      may not have been apple.

Despite the Persian word

         for apple

beginning with sin,

    apples originate from Xinjiang,

which is a great distance

      from the Garden of Eden

if that's not far off our mark,

       so the catalytic fruit

is thought to have been a fig

    although whatever figment

of pride could suppose

   knowledge of prelapsarian geography

not to mention botany

       betrays the fruit pit

we have swallowed.

     I like to speculate nevertheless

that it was a quince

   that gave us our quirk of knowledge,

if only because Adam

     biting into one with gusto,

almost chipping a tooth,

    embodies the bicuspid of truth.

I like the folk wisdom

    that the way to pick a quince

is to put a hand beneath

      a promising fruit

and lift it sideways;

     if it slides off in your hand

it's ripe –

  which would raise all sorts of questions

about arboreal design.

      Absolute divinity

could build to blueprint

     so this would bear out

what would have always been part

    of the plan. Most of all,

Adam would not have known

      that he needed

to cook the misshapen pulp

        to make it palatable

until he had ingested it,

        which seems to me delicious irony,

much as the raw aroma

        of rose and guava and honey

would have been as irresistible

        as the flavour impenetrable.

Only after the fact

        would he know to start a fire

and simmer the fruit

        until it softens

and the pectins leach out

        to form its own preserve.

Yet, holding a density of fruit

        with shape and definition

makes it reducible

        and not through regression

if not perfectly so,

        and that sweet process

is one you can make what you will of,

        whether

a paste or a jelly,

        but however you prepare it

that candied sweetness

        and being conscious of that sweetness

is the bar to happiness,

        the base of never being at rest

for how much more there is to go:

        a distance beyond measure,

like casting off on an ocean voyage

        and looking for a sight of land

as every day that passes

        doubles the probable time

to reach the other side,

        that undefined tropical shore

lush with breadfruit and pineapple,

        the length and breadth of paradise.

Airborne
for Sid Gómez Hildawa (1962–2008)

I

To be bent
                    over a styrofoam omelette
trying to
            decide whether
                                to switch
hands on the plastic knife
                            for dishwater
coffee
            is not the best time
                                to be hearing
an inflight announcement
                            of an emergency
in seat 40A and that
                        any passenger who is
a doctor should
                    please make himself known.

Of course it's a worse time
                                for seat 40A,
but for
            the cabin
                        razoring the troposphere
not to know
            what transpires
                                is to stare out
over the dark
                topographical
                                scarring below
with no sense
                of whose villages
and landscapes
                    we would be crashing upon
if something
            happens.

Instead I gaze out
               on the moon,
                              pale
as goat's cheese
               yet luminous,
                              encircled,
throwing a portion of itself
                              upon the wing
now slippery
               and metallic.
                              It is only
as day breaks
               and the sun
                              casts
uneven shadows
               on the ailerons
                              that I
notice
        black specks
                      in the porthole
between
           the outer
                      and inner glass.
How they got there
                    will remain
a vanilla mystery
                    dispersed by the spread
of fernleaf ice
               and, below us,
the snake of the Thames,
                          the notches
of Canary Wharf,
                  and further out
                                  still
the Home Counties,
                    misted
                           as a sea.

II

Out on the balcony
                    the rain is pattering
with the light
                    insistence of a friend,
out there
          in the deepening dusk
                              made hollow
by stillness
              after a passage
                              of wind.
At such times
                it is difficult
                              to be definite
about where it is
                  the boundaries lie
to be measured out
                    and chalked up
by the length
              of a breath.

Whatever you touch
                    at such uneven times
becomes part
              of a cadence
                          that extends
beyond you,
            that takes in
                          parquet flooring,
fruit bowl,
            pinewood table;
                            takes hold of you
as much as
            dandelion seeds
                            are borne
by the winds
              that they represent.

One day
        long ago now,
                      you know not when,

you heard the calling
                    of a peregrinatory wind
carrying the scent
                    of ripe sea
                                and damp earth,
and lightly made
                    a compact
                                with that spirit,
that if it would take you
                    where it went
you would replace
                    each leaf
                                that it disturbed.
You did not know
                    this was
                                no ordinary breath
you could cut short
                    by weeping,
                                until,
self-eddied
                    in the slipstream
                                of its sweep
you could not keep up,
                    and the trees grew bare
and all the leaves
                    of all the books
                                you turned
turned out
                    to leave you forever
                                in their dust.
You wind up sitting,
                    slackly,
                                in this desolation
of innumerable upturned boats
                    sapped and slowly
browning
                    before your eyes.
                                Sometimes they stir
in vortices
                    as your old adversary
                                taunts you,

pretending to be living
                    among the living,
in your physics,
                in your paths
                            and in your time.
Your father once told you
                        never to race
against the wind
                but always with it.
If you listen,
            you can hear
                        his autumnal whisper.

III

From the porthole
                I can see
a lightning storm
                scant miles
                            to my right.
It is like
            seeing clearly for
                        milliseconds
as blue flashes
            illuminate
                        and outline
with sudden nuance
                the soft-centred clouds.

All the substance of dream
                        exactly concentrates
in those moments
                one hopes to catch,
                            which leave
a sweet taste
            and no
                    memory of themselves.
In those moments
                are angels,
                        eternity,

tiny histories
                    reforming fractally
                                        into
our brand of strife,
                    our innumerable nerves.
The wish to cage
                    lightning
                                        is the cramped urge
for a map
                    to the lines
                                        crossing taut bodies,
and the means but
                    chords
                                        on a piano,
chords that bind us
                    more than we imagine,
our tendinous chords,
                    our papillary muscles,
our ventricles
                    that push out
                                        submerged air
into purpling
                    thirst.
                                        You can only see this
from a distance:
                    the fist of clouds,
those leakages
                    of light,
                                        twitching electricity.
We do not know
                    how cold it is
                                        out there
beyond factoried
                    instruments
                                        charting
trembling trajectories
                    that cannot bridge
your cold
                    that has become
                                        our cold.

You tried
          to cross the river
                    but the current
was too strong,
          and now you are borne
by a different
          current,
                    born into the midst
of those who inhabit
               the accelerating edges,
the illusive day sky,
          the lightness of air.

JAN WAGNER was born in Hamburg in 1971. He has published four volumes of poetry, including *Achtzehn Pasteten* (Eighteen Pastries, 2007) and *Australien* (2010), as well as a volume of essays, *Die Sandale des Propheten* (The Prophet's Sandal, 2011). His latest book, *Die Eulenhasser in den Hallenhäusern* (The Owl Haters in the Hall Houses), appeared in 2012. He is a translator of American and British poetry and co-editor of the anthology *Lyrik von Jetzt* (Poetry of Now). He lives in Berlin.

IAIN GALBRAITH has translated many German and Austrian poets into English, including Esther Dischereit, Ulrike Draesner, Michael Donhauser, Raoul Schrott, Alfred Kolleritsch and W.G. Sebald. His own poems have appeared in *The Times Literary Supplement*, *Poetry Review*, *New Writing*, and *PN Review*. He lives in Wiesbaden, Germany.

Grateful acknowledgement is made to Berlin Verlag (Berlin) for permission to publish the translations of poems from *Guerickes Sperling*, *Achtzehn Pasteten* and *Australien*.

A good poem can pool the maximum of linguistic resources in the smallest of fields, harmonising opposites and paradoxes, allowing them to chime, amplifying musicality and meaning. It will also uphold the fundamental poetic virtues of surprise and transgression (whether in violating conventions of its own making or rules imposed from without), granting the greatest possible freedom in the most compact space.

A poem can be wrought out of anything. Objects that are ordinary enough to be overlooked in everyday life may suddenly reveal unforeseen poetic dimensions. The attempt to write a poem about freedom itself may come to nothing, while concentrating on a white glove that somebody has dropped in the gutter may lead to an outstanding poem about freedom.

I am interested in the tension between form, which is always of the essence in poetry, and the poem's more ludic qualities. Impure rhymes and other devices can subvert the rigidity of fixed verse forms without exposing them to ridicule. Each of the latter has its own allure – the sestina with its game of sixes, the villanelle with its pattern of repetitions. These need not be felt as restrictions. On the contrary, to reject such forms when their peculiarities might benefit a poem would, in my view, amount to a forfeiting of freedom. A formal corset can facilitate breathing, if it is conceived less in terms of an obligation than as a process encouraging the imagery and thought of a poem to set out in a new or unanticipated direction.

The striking, original quality of a successful poem lies in its ability to grasp or say something that has not been put in the same way before, while making it seem perfectly natural to do so – as if, in the past, people had simply neglected to see things in the right light, while knowing instinctively that such a way of seeing must exist. Such a poem will be unpretentious, while drawing on unlimited resources; multi-layered, but not gratuitously so. A good poem will show an awareness of the medium, of the potential and limits of its language, and it will do so without being explicit or compromising its sensuality – its bond with our steaming, glowing, odorous, noisy world. Without that bond, it can never become what Dylan Thomas meant when he described the poem as a contribution to reality. And that is just what my next, as yet unwritten poem will attempt to be – for isn't there always that one poem waiting to be written? Everything urges us to write it.

anomalies

impossible to trace the note back to its author,
for keeping mum was thought a point of honour,
and yet the news was plain – herr richter
had three nipples. a tinkling peel of laughter
passed along the row of girls behind us
and died like showering pins. beyond the window:
early christmas snow. a train in the distance
was splitting the white sky from the white below
when the bell brought us up with a jolt:
in the corridor on endless shelves, afloat
in their heavens of formaldehyde,
were tiny naked gods – each dewy eye
watched us walking past. as if they knew what
growth lowered under our skin, and why.

columbus

there stands columbus, lost in thought,
the board an empty space, and in the court
the maple's green sail, the clatter and clamour
of genoa. a breeze blows from the harbour
where the sailors gabble on about antillia,
the abject leper exposes his stigmata
like a *mappemonde*'s white birthmarks,
while hawsers left in heaps out on the mole flex,
coiling in their sleep, and the kelp's script
is dissolved, rewritten, rubbed out –
as if the sea were still at school, a classmate
of columbus, who even now receives a clout
about the lugs from his preceptor, so hard
the earth begins to shift beneath his feet.

december 1914

'One of the nuts belonging to the regiment got out of the trenches and
started to walk towards the German lines.'

'course we thought they'd gone loco,
each man-jack a sitting duck
armed with naught but mistletoe
and plum-pud. but they were in luck –

the guns were still. in no-man's-land
and mud we met between the lines,
at a loss for words, each hand
at a trouser seam, until the woodbines

did the rounds, were lit, and someone
shared a bar of bitter chocolate.
one man had news of a poison
that did away with louse and rat,

others, still too stiff to talk, swigged
rum, or got out family photos,
played halma, yelled, swapped
addresses, uniforms, helmets, jocose

till under the sheaves of streaking tracer
on that soft and naked common field
there was nothing left to offer
but the trenches and their nameless yield.

tea bag

I
draped only in a
sackcloth mantle. the little
hermit in his cave.

II
a single thread leads
to the upper world. we shall
give him five minutes.

from *'eighteen pastries'*

shepherd's pie

sheep are clouds who love the ground.
the shepherd's in love with marie. scatters
nuts on the slope, whispers the three famous words.
the flock bleats, gobbling them up like white script
on a green board. bounding behind comes dot,
the sheepdog. in windows down in the valley
they draw the evening shadows. they
don't see the slope or the hill, nor the clouds:
clouds that are sheep the wind has found.

pâté chaud de harengs aux pommes de terre

when, clutching at his left breast, joost the fisher
staggered, we all knew what was wrong: his heart.
he had gone to sea, they said, on a freighter
as a young man – a renowned chaser of skirt,

so the story went, a drinker, and the sea
ran blue, the wind went where it listed. he stayed
mum. even when the cups weren't filled with tea
and the talk flowed, his pipe's red eye wouldn't fade;

and just when you'd start to think he was warming
and a flicker of something appeared to lurk
on his lips, he spoke only of the swarming
shoals deep down. that thrashing fin in the dark.

cheese and onion pastries

I have a heart of stone, men say,
but what do they know about stones.

– Maria Barnas

what i know about stones is their weight
in the bellies of wolves; and that after falling
into the belly of a well they will echo;
or how they seemed to ponder, one may night

on the side of a hill, bathed in moonlight,
pale as onions. but of onions what do i know,
apart from their skin frocks and their sting,
and layer by layer their retiring heart.

the west

the river thinks in fish. what was it then
that sergeant henley was the first to wrest
from its grasp, its eyes staring yellow, its barbels
two poker hooks around an ash-grey mouth
that made even our dogs whimper?

we are following the rapids and their
raging grammar to the source.
the distant haze of mountains,
grassy plains, and now and then
a native throwing an amused look
in our direction only to vanish
in the forest: all this we enter
on adam's ancient map, naming
species and deeds. fever in our muscles
and week after week a diet of roots
and trust in god. under our shirts tics
like pearl-headed pins in our skin:
the wilderness taking our measure.

strange feeling being
the frontier, the point of ending
and beginning. at night by the fire our blood
circles above us in clouds of mosquitoes
while we sew the hides together
with hard fish-bones: shoes
for our destination, blankets for our dreams.
before us untouched land, behind us
the raving settlers, their charter
of fences and gates; behind us
the covered wagons of traders,
the big towns, full of noise and future.

the man from the sea

they find him in a dinner suit of salt
and sand, his passport seaweed, an ensemble
of herring gulls behind him in the drizzle.

he says nothing, but lets the surging felt-
surf caper through the piano case
to great surprise. the heavy epaulettes
of hands weigh on his shoulders: this
is his hour of fame, an era of tablets

on autumn nights, when the nurses float
like icebergs through the corridors. in the clinic
garden the last leaves flutter
beneath the walls. from an old cabin,
ivy-covered, rides the muted tinkle
of a piano. some think it's chopin.

staniszów

where we stayed under fruit trees.
where with the green claws of lizards
ivy scaled the walls of the palace,
the aged stared into their fishponds
as if into photo albums. the leaves
falling in the park. a brown trout
making a leap for the next chapter.

where all evening behind the white
moon of a lampshade circling moths
purred with the workings of their wings –
the panicked numbers of a clock.
days in the slow month of august
and a final frothing of flowerbeds.
later, drumming on the roof of the car,
apples, small and hard, like children's fists.

blues in august
for Kevin Young

august is so empty, the rooms are full
of clocks, and they are all too slow:
      august is so empty.
the breeze steps in through my window to touch
the plants, see if all is still, and go.

august is so distant, the lofty sail
we loved was yesterday's azure:
      august is so distant.
we wait for a letter to perch on our hand,
a snowy bird to bring us news of shore.

august is so gloomy, the moon this pale
and watchful face above my desk:
      august is so gloomy.
and out on the streets those passing taxis
smuggle their bars of gold through the dusk.

dobermann
for Ron Winkler

this is the village, and this the master
knacker's dwelling, a wisp of smoke
snaking skyward from the roof.

the empty hides on the walls. a basket
of pups, their eyes still sutured
by blindness, taking their first sniff

of the world. it is early, cartographers and land
surveyors in the towns are still abed.
that well in the garden brims with thirst.

apolda, thuringia: the dead cow
at the edge of the field is a grounded balloon,
bloated with plague. it will lie there

a while yet. he strides out under the small
coin of the stars. and at his side
the two black blades keep slicing through the fields.

chameleon

older than the pastoral staff
it drags along behind it, its crook
of a tail. come down, we call
to it on its branch, while its telescope
tongue snaps out to consume
a dragonfly constellation: an astronomer
gazing at once at the sky
and the ground, keeping his distance
from both. the dome of its eye, armour-
plated with scales, is a fortress. only
a pupil moves within, an edgy
flicker behind the arrow-slit (sometimes
you'll find its skin, like some deserted
outpost or long-discarded theory).
come down, we call. but it doesn't
budge, vanishing slowly among
the colours. hiding itself in the world.

hops

ungainly at first,
they are like calves tottering on spindly legs,
abandoned to foreign soil.

until the wires pull them up –
then they climb, and their leaves grow rough
and calloused, the edges armed with teeth.

no rest for them
until they are metres high, and finding expression
in cones that are small and yellow and bitter.

by july they are an army camp, ensconced
in the hills, silent under their green.
all at once, overnight, they're gone,

and only their flagless poles remain.
the moon wind in the bare villages
carries the roar of the taverns across the land.

meteorite

in your garden, perhaps,
between the tomato vines
and the carrots, just as
you're getting the coffee on

and recalling the farmer who ran
outside, hearing a burglar,
to stare out through a hole in the roof of his barn
into the circle of an older

flashlight, the verger who instead
of daffodils
discovered a lump of black, a foundling left
on the threshold with the chuckle

of youthful heavens deep inside it,
cattle lowing in pain in the dawn,
the milk gone sour, a man coming out
of a café to find a ton

of scrap-metal his car-key still fits –
or that it was always the beginning
of some cult, or the moment the plague sets
in, on a monday morning

when the neighbour's dog suddenly
starts to bark and you go to the door
somewhat older, but hardly
old, and no place else but here.

All poems translated by Iain Galbraith

KAREN MCCARTHY WOOLF was born in London to English and Jamaican parents, and is Writer in Residence at the November Project, a tidal energy initiative on the Thames. Her poetry and criticism have appeared in *Poetry Review*, *Poetry London* and *Modern Poetry in Translation*; her collection *An Aviary of Small Birds* is forthcoming from OxfordPoets.

I think poetry is a place where we seek to resolve everyday or philosophical quandaries – about who we are and how we fit in to the bigger picture. Writing poems gives me the space to think disruptively (rather than logically), shake things up a bit and restore some form of balance, not necessarily in a linear fashion but definitely in an intuitive manner. I'm very interested in how our emotional and intellectual impulses intersect and for me, poetry is the art form best suited to this endeavour. As a reader and writer, I want a poem to transmit feelings and ideas in equal measure.

The sequence included here is part of an ongoing conversation I have with the natural world as a writer. I've always been fascinated by our societal relationship with the moon: it's a phenomenon that crosses many different cultures and analytical perspectives, whether theological, scientific or folkloric. Many ancient civilisations – from the Americas to Asia, Africa and pre-Christian Europe – had names for the moon in each of its phases, which would in turn relate to the season. The moon controls tides and affects growing seasons, it determines when females menstruate and, famously, as the many werewolf transformation myths underscore, it affects our moods.

I love the idea of the moon as a character, with whims and peculiarities of her own. That's part of what's behind the poem 'Blue' – I was captivated by the thought of what might happen when the moon herself was on a downer. The clowns whose job it is to cheer her up are based on the Lakota 'Heyokha' – sacred clowns who healed with laughter and whose societal position was similar to that of the European court jester.

Naming is also one of my little obsessions as a writer: how the names we choose for places, people, objects, tell stories about where we come from and how we relate to our environment. It's also a deeply political act that speaks as much about ownership as it does identification.

As a whole, this sequence sits within a group of elegies in my collection *An Aviary of Small Birds* concerning the loss of a baby son in childbirth. As such, the moon's latent connection to fertility also relates to another more personal cycle of pregnancy, birth, loss and transcendence.

Thirteen Names for the Moon

I: SNOW

Her word is an ocean
of almond blossom
blown in under the door
by gales that
bang shutters
against plastered walls.

II: WINTER

All her seas run dry
        and marrow dark;

though the Sea of Crises
overflows
        month after month.

III: WOLF

Turmeric-eyed and luminous,
el día lunes, Monday too,
lupine, *la lune, la una* and
alone.
She is never alone.

IV: ICE

Unexploited frozen reservoirs are
concealed under a polar nipple that
burns with pinpricks.

A probe is programmed to crash
into a shadowed crater in accordance with
The Outer Space Treaty (last time
she checked she hadn't signed).

There's water here, more than we've left
in the Sahara. If only it would melt.
Silver, sulphur, mercury and methane
are also unexpectedly unearthed
and now there's scope for future colonies.

Viewed from the observation platform
her solidified lakes shine like duck eggs.

V: CROW

And so the story goes...
white birds with black blood
cast shadows as they
touch down at Mumbai Airport
while Crow flies low
over baggage reclaim –
He drops a molten marble into the sky,
            gets the ball rolling...

VI: EGG

An avocado stone
is planted, watered, watched
until its roots touch
the edge of the pot,
its cool clay belly.

She wants all the eggs
to synchronise
with the swell and fall
of moods, subtle
as the tides she charms
then spurns
as she elongates
the globe
into a watery
ovoid.

VII: HARE

Rabbit kits grow commensurate
with her wane and wax

while the leveret embryo
is more Lenten:

it takes approximately forty days
for a litter to emerge, fully furred,

from the capsule of the womb,
eyes already open.

The does are her familiars.
In the mating season

they rear up
and box with the bucks,

the last left standing mounts.
We see one flash into the woods

on the hill behind the house –
        mistake it for a deer.

Her ears are everywhere:
the motorway's waterfall of noise

floods the morning, a train shrieks
at a teenage copse whose saplings

rush to their rooms and slam doors
over the crackle of fickle pylons,

another SMS pulses, thrushes
and finches pipe louder…

> *All this screech!*
> *Bring me instead*
> *the copper urn and a rifle*
> *so I can shoot*
> *a lurcher for the pot.*

Did you know soft pellets are nibbled
direct from the anus?

No nourishment is wasted.
The digestive tract is calibrated finely.

Always alert she knows
how to lie low, stomach pressed

to ridges of churned soil.
Trap her and she'll kick hard enough

to break her own back.
The only way for her to live is wild.

VIII: NECTAR

She is a perfect circle, her face round
as a pill stamped with the contours
of a dove who flies through a recurring dream
she had in the last days of the twentieth century,
where her non-existent lover flounders
in the prickly basalt of the Marsh of Sleep.
He wants her to fish him out, fling him
to her obedient groves where oranges cluster
like fledgling planets around the base
of tree trunks and honeysuckle garlands
his curls, rampant as knotweed, its trumpet
flowers sweet as jam on a cracker.
But first you've got to come up to the castle,
make a move or two on the dance floor,
feel the bass thump as you trampoline
to yet another daybreak where blacked-up
Morris men sport pheasant feathers in sawn-off
top hats, clash sticks, knock wood and suddenly
the sky's a swimming pool where every colour's
brighter, yes you love the taste of gin
at 9 a.m. when chunks of ice dissolve in its fizz
and now you know what love is
and have to wear unconjugated sunglasses
to offset the dazzle she only reflects,

let's not forget, as her glitter rushes and she turns
and twirls and at no time do you ever
stop.

IX: THUNDER

Her prophecies adorn the bedside table:
an orb of black roses, their scent metallic
as the clash of swords and shields
when the lights flicker in the museum's long,
glassy corridors where totems topple
and display cabinets splinter with fright.

On the bench in the hospital garden
endorphins invade my arteries
as microscopic pearls, involuntarily
suckled from a celestial breast.
A nurse doses me
with a hormone to plug my milk ducts.

X: DOG

It is the time when all things ripen:
corn swells to teeth in the husk,
rivers pant in summer's heat
and the little streams are exhausted.

Who says your death is blameless?
I want to slip this August moon in a sack
and watch her wriggle like a puppy
as she's swallowed by the lake.

XI: HARVEST

Even a star
      must share
      the sky with the Earth.

The horizon belongs to neither west nor east.

Nothing seems to sate
      us; we scramble arse
      over tit & hate
to save
anything we can have.

If tears
were prayed-for rain we'd still starve.

XII: BLUE

The clown has a power that comes from the thunder beings, not from the
animals or the earth. Being a clown gives you honour but also shame.
It brings you power, but you have to pay for it.

                                   – Lame Deer

Le Général keeps a silver shovel
in a Persian carpet bag; loves

a bad-boy rumble
down the hill in hot-rod prams.

His men pull old accordions out of hats,
an icy christening cake is smashed

in scars and face, an elbow in my soup
Sir! Bonnets big and white as parachutes.

Hankies flap like elephant ears, bare
cheeks rouged, tattooed with tear

drops. A cavalry of spoons on knees,
bouncy bedsprings, laceless shoes.

How to cheer our Lady up they ask?
Face the firing squad. It's die or laugh.

Initiation's a crawl through fire.
Two years ago a mutt was boiled alive.

If soothing lullaby or harp don't work
then lightning quick like sharks

they make their move and strike;
advantage is their art's surprise.

What poxy dose of mathematics!
Every now and then she gets like this.

XIII: BLOOD

Death is out hunting tonight, the moon
is a torch in his hand – deer, bears,
boar, babies… Sugar skulls and swaddled
loaves are offered up for *los angelitos*
while songbirds dart, pick strands
of flesh from between his teeth
their music constant as he strides.

Of course it doesn't really go like this:
the doctor wastes
twenty minutes trying to scrape
a blood sample from your scalp.
By the time they slice me open it's too late.
Blood-splashed plastic aprons are binned
with pointless sharps.

… Yet still, my love, I long for you,
as the two caged canaries
who hop and whirr
from the blue plastic perch
to the cone-shaped nest, coiled from wire
and filled with unfertilised eggs,
long for the ravine.